Contents

How to use this book

Multiplying

Each page has a title telling you what it is about.

Hint: You might calculate like this, or you might choose another method.

1.	4	0·5	0·06	1·2·0
	3	1·2	1·5·0·18	1·5
			+	0·18
				1·3·68

This shows how to set out your work.

This Hint will help you to answer the question.

£8·72   £1·98

£4·56   £3·68

£5·74   £7·85   £2·75

Write the cost of:

1. 3 pairs of gloves
2. 4 bobble hats
3. 5 pairs of shorts
4. 8 T-shirts
5. 3 caps
6. 6 pairs of flip-flops
7. 8 pairs of socks
8. 4 pairs each of socks and gloves

Instructions look like this. Always read these carefully before starting.

You can buy any two items. Investigate how many of each you can buy with £30.

These are Rocket activities. Ask your teacher if you need to do these questions.

Complete these multiplications.

9. $3 \times 1·26 =$
10. $4 \times 2·57 =$
11. $5 \times 4·36 =$
12. $8 \times 7·42 =$
13. $9 \times 3·87 =$
14. $4 \times 8·64 =$
15. $7 \times 3·92 =$
16. $6 \times 4·38 =$
17. $9 \times 5·28 =$

76   I can multiply with tenths and hundredths

Read this to check you understand what you have been learning on the page.

Mixed numbers and improper fractions

How many cakes?

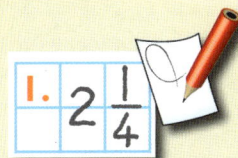

1. $2\frac{1}{4}$

1

2

3

4

5

6

7

8

9

There were five of each kind of cake. How much has been eaten each time?

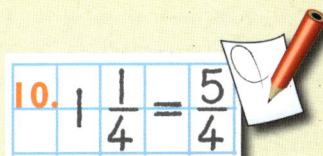

10. $1\frac{1}{4} = \frac{5}{4}$

How many quarters?

10 $1\frac{1}{4}$

11 $2\frac{3}{4}$

12 $3\frac{1}{4}$

13 5

How many thirds?

14 $1\frac{2}{3}$

15 $3\frac{1}{3}$

16 $5\frac{2}{3}$

17 3

How many fifths?

18 $1\frac{3}{5}$

19 $2\frac{1}{5}$

20 $3\frac{4}{5}$

21 $6\frac{3}{5}$

I can give examples of improper fractions and of mixed numbers

Mixed numbers and improper fractions

Write the number of bars of chocolate.

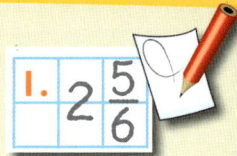

1. $2\frac{5}{6}$

1

2

3

4

5

6

7

8

9

Write the number of:

thirds

| 10 | $2\frac{1}{3}$ | 11 | $3\frac{1}{3}$ | 12 | $5\frac{2}{3}$ |

quarters

| 13 | $4\frac{1}{4}$ | 14 | $1\frac{3}{4}$ | 15 | $7\frac{2}{4}$ |

fifths

| 16 | $6\frac{4}{5}$ | 17 | $4\frac{3}{5}$ | 18 | $5\frac{2}{5}$ |

tenths

| 19 | $1\frac{3}{10}$ | 20 | $3\frac{1}{10}$ | 21 | $2\frac{7}{10}$ |

sixths

| 22 | $1\frac{1}{6}$ | 23 | $1\frac{5}{6}$ | 24 | $3\frac{5}{6}$ |

Explore writing, as mixed fractions, the number of hours in 100, 150, 200… minutes. Now try the number of weeks in 10, 20, 30 days.

I can give examples of improper fractions and of mixed numbers

Mixed numbers and improper fractions

Write each as a mixed number.

1. $1\frac{1}{2}$

1 $\frac{3}{2}$ 2 $\frac{4}{3}$ 3 $\frac{7}{4}$ 4 $\frac{13}{10}$

5 $\frac{13}{5}$ 6 $\frac{21}{8}$ 7 $\frac{17}{7}$ 8 $\frac{50}{6}$

Use number cards 2–8.

Choose two cards to make an improper fraction that can also be written as a mixed number.

Watch out! $\frac{6}{2}$ will not do, because it cannot make a mixed number.

How many improper fractions like this can you make?

Write the number of towers of each height.

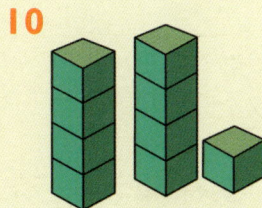

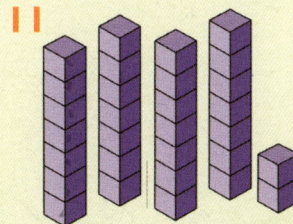

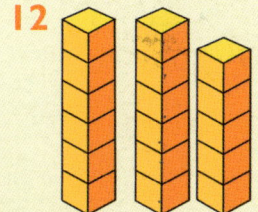

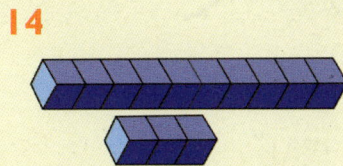

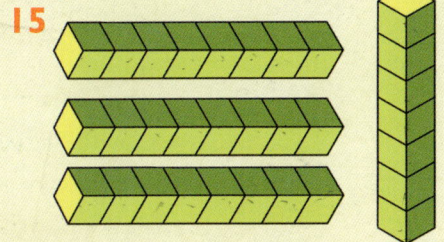

9. $2\frac{3}{5}$

9   10   11   12

13   14   15

I can explain what improper fractions and mixed numbers are and can give examples of both

Mixed numbers and improper fractions

Write each as an improper fraction.

$$1. \quad 4\frac{1}{3} = \frac{13}{3}$$

1. $4\frac{1}{3}$
2. $5\frac{2}{5}$
3. $1\frac{3}{4}$
4. $6\frac{4}{5}$

5. $2\frac{7}{8}$
6. $1\frac{7}{10}$
7. $3\frac{5}{7}$
8. $1\frac{5}{6}$

9. $4\frac{3}{8}$
10. $11\frac{2}{3}$
11. $14\frac{1}{4}$
12. $8\frac{5}{9}$

13. $3\frac{8}{12}$
14. $7\frac{5}{11}$
15. $12\frac{5}{9}$
16. $6\frac{13}{15}$

Use 1–10 number cards.
Choose two cards to create an improper fraction that can also be written as a mixed number.
Record your numbers.
Do this several times. What is the highest mixed number you can make? And the lowest?

Write the missing numbers.

17. $1\frac{3}{5} = \frac{\square}{5}$

18. $2\frac{\square}{7} = \frac{18}{7}$

19. $3\frac{2}{3} = \frac{\square}{3}$

20. $5\frac{\square}{9} = \frac{49}{9}$

21. $\square\frac{3}{8} = \frac{51}{8}$

22. $\square\frac{3}{4} = \frac{19}{4}$

23. $8\frac{7}{10} = \frac{\square}{10}$

24. $2\frac{\square}{6} = \frac{17}{6}$

25. $\square\frac{1}{2} = \frac{9}{2}$

26. $7\frac{4}{5} = \frac{\square}{5}$

27. $5\frac{\square}{3} = \frac{17}{3}$

28. $\square\frac{2}{15} = \frac{47}{15}$

I can change mixed numbers to improper fractions

Mixed numbers and improper fractions

Write <, > or = between each pair.

$1. \ 3\frac{1}{2} < \frac{9}{2}$

1   $3\frac{1}{2}$ and $\frac{9}{2}$ 2 $4\frac{2}{3}$ and $\frac{16}{3}$ 3 $\frac{27}{4}$ and $5\frac{3}{4}$

4   $\frac{21}{5}$ and $3\frac{4}{5}$ 5 $3\frac{7}{10}$ and $\frac{31}{10}$ 6 $\frac{23}{6}$ and $3\frac{5}{6}$

7   $\frac{38}{7}$ and $5\frac{2}{7}$ 8 $\frac{59}{9}$ and $6\frac{7}{9}$ 9 $4\frac{3}{8}$ and $\frac{31}{8}$ 10 $2\frac{5}{12}$ and $\frac{29}{12}$

Change each set to mixed numbers, then write them in order, smallest to largest:

11   $\frac{7}{3}, \frac{7}{4}, \frac{5}{2}, \frac{21}{5}, \frac{53}{10}$ 12 $\frac{23}{6}, \frac{21}{5}, \frac{27}{10}, \frac{16}{3}, \frac{27}{4}$

13   $\frac{8}{9}, \frac{10}{7}, \frac{14}{3}, \frac{29}{8}, \frac{14}{5}$ 14 $\frac{33}{4}, \frac{38}{7}, \frac{38}{9}, \frac{63}{10}, \frac{13}{8}$

15   $\frac{11}{4}, \frac{23}{3}, \frac{17}{5}, \frac{9}{2}, \frac{35}{6}$ 16 $\frac{24}{5}, \frac{18}{7}, \frac{17}{10}, \frac{29}{4}, \frac{26}{3}$

Write a set of improper fractions whose mixed numbers are between 5 and 10.

I am a fraction. Who am I?

17   My numerator and denominator have a total of 7. I am between $\frac{1}{2}$ and 1.

18   My denominator is double my numerator. I am a number of sixths.

19   I am between 2 and 3 and my denominator is 2.

20   My numerator and denominator have a total of 10. I am between 2 and 3.

Equivalent Fractions

In each pair of pictures, the shaded fractions match.
Write the fractions.

1. $\dfrac{1}{2} = \dfrac{2}{4}$

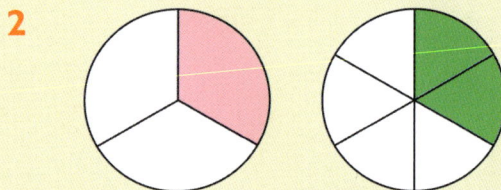

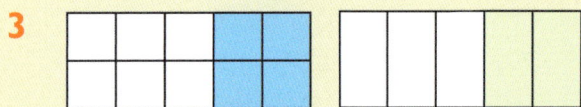

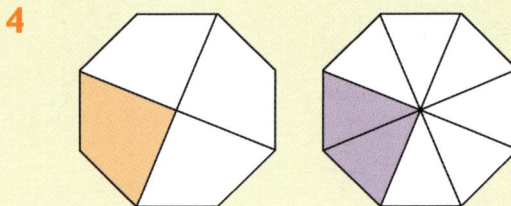

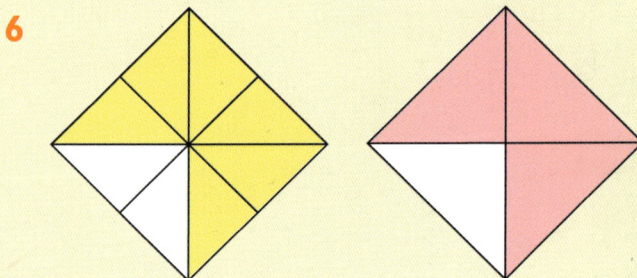

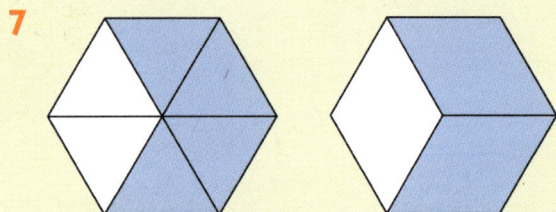

1

2

3

4

5

6

7

8

Write the pairs of unshaded fractions.

2. $\dfrac{2}{3} = \dfrac{4}{6}$

Draw your own grid. Shade half,
then write the equivalent fractions.
How many different grids can you draw?

$\dfrac{3}{6} = \dfrac{1}{2}$

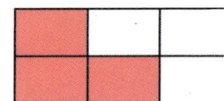

I can find fractions that are equal

Equivalent Fractions

1 Find pairs where the fractions shaded are the same. Write the pairs and their fractions.

$$\text{1. } a, \quad g: \frac{4}{8} = \frac{1}{2}$$

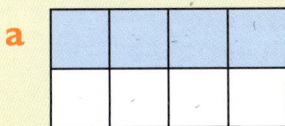

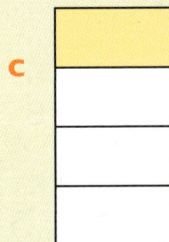

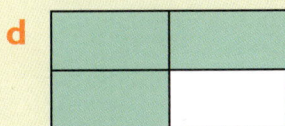

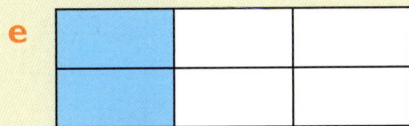

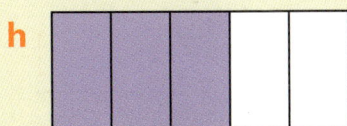

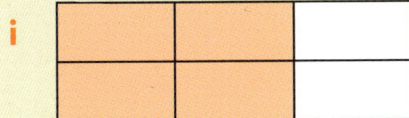

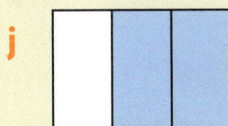

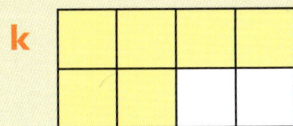

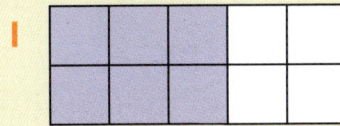

a

b

c

d

e

f   g

h

i

j

k

l

2 Add two more different pairs of your own.

Use number cards 1 – 8.

Make some pairs of equivalent fractions.

When fractions match, what do you notice about the pattern of numerators and denominators?

How many matches can you find?
How many more can you make if you add cards 9 and 10?

$$\frac{\square}{\square} = \frac{\square}{\square}$$

$$\frac{2}{3} = \frac{4}{6}$$

Equivalent Fractions

Complete these pairs of equivalent fractions. Use the fraction walls to help you.

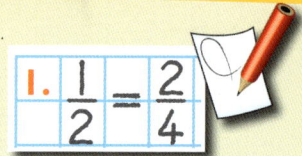

1. $\frac{1}{2} = \frac{2}{4}$

1 $\frac{1}{2} = \frac{\Box}{4}$

2 $\frac{2}{4} = \frac{\Box}{8}$

3 $\frac{2}{2} = \frac{\Box}{4}$

4 $\frac{6}{8} = \frac{\Box}{4}$

5 $\frac{1}{2} = \frac{\Box}{8}$

6 $1 = \frac{\Box}{4}$

7 $\frac{1}{3} = \frac{\Box}{6}$

8 $\frac{\Box}{3} = \frac{4}{6}$

9 $\frac{3}{6} = \frac{\Box}{12}$

10 $\frac{\Box}{3} = \frac{8}{12}$

11 $\frac{1}{3} = \frac{\Box}{12}$

12 $\frac{\Box}{3} = \frac{6}{6}$

1			
$\frac{1}{2}$		$\frac{1}{2}$	
$\frac{1}{4}$	$\frac{1}{4}$	$\frac{1}{4}$	$\frac{1}{4}$
$\frac{1}{8}$ $\frac{1}{8}$	$\frac{1}{8}$ $\frac{1}{8}$	$\frac{1}{8}$ $\frac{1}{8}$	$\frac{1}{8}$ $\frac{1}{8}$

1		
$\frac{1}{3}$	$\frac{1}{3}$	$\frac{1}{3}$
$\frac{1}{6}$ $\frac{1}{6}$	$\frac{1}{6}$ $\frac{1}{6}$	$\frac{1}{6}$ $\frac{1}{6}$
$\frac{1}{12}$ $\frac{1}{12}$ $\frac{1}{12}$ $\frac{1}{12}$	$\frac{1}{12}$ $\frac{1}{12}$ $\frac{1}{12}$ $\frac{1}{12}$	$\frac{1}{12}$ $\frac{1}{12}$ $\frac{1}{12}$ $\frac{1}{12}$

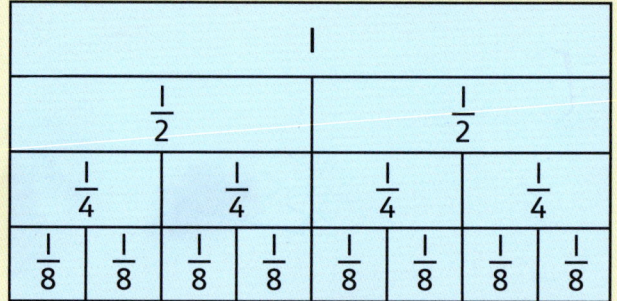

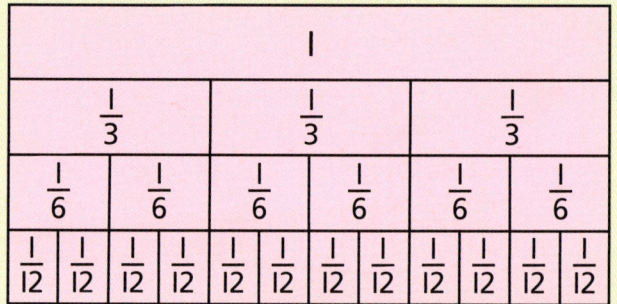

The bottom of my fraction wall is divided into $\frac{1}{20}$ s. Draw the whole wall.

13 There were 16 cyclists on a trip. Half of them stay in a hostel, and a quarter of them camp. How many go home for the night?

14 Class 4 has 30 children. Half have packed lunches. One sixth go home. What fraction have school dinners? How many children is this?

15 James had 12 marbles. Two sixths were red, one third were blue, the rest were green. What fraction was green?

I can find fractions that are equal

Equivalent Fractions

For each set of pictures, write a set of equivalent fractions.

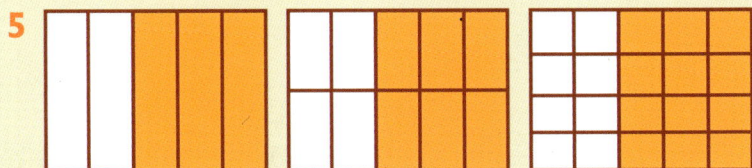

$$1. \frac{1}{2}, \frac{2}{4} \ldots$$

1

2

3

4

5

Find the equivalent fractions. Use the 10 × 10 square to help you.

6 $\frac{60}{100} = \frac{\square}{10}$

7 $\frac{1}{2} = \frac{\square}{10}$

8 $\frac{1}{2} = \frac{\square}{100}$

9 $\frac{10}{100} = \frac{\square}{10}$

10 $\frac{9}{10} = \frac{\square}{100}$

11 $\frac{1}{4} = \frac{\square}{100}$

12 $\frac{3}{4} = \frac{\square}{100}$

13 $\frac{4}{10} = \frac{\square}{100}$

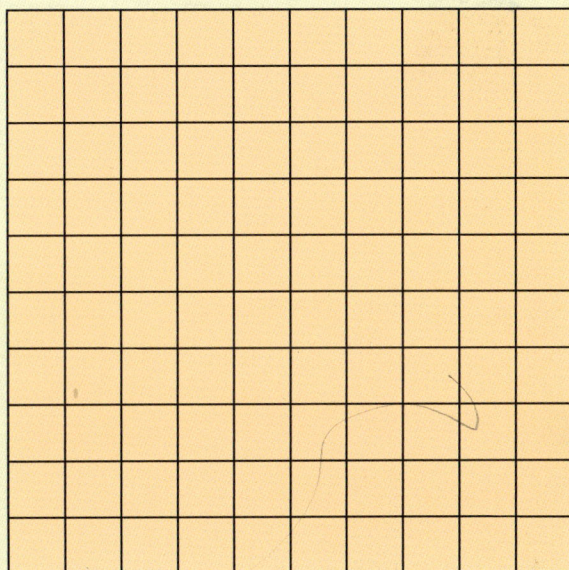

Write equivalent fractions for each of $\frac{1}{10}, \frac{2}{10}, \ldots \frac{10}{10}$.
Can you write some for twentieths?

I can use pictures to help me find fractions that are equal

Equivalent Fractions

Copy and complete. Use the lines to help you.

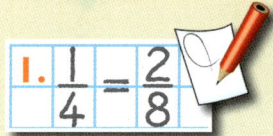

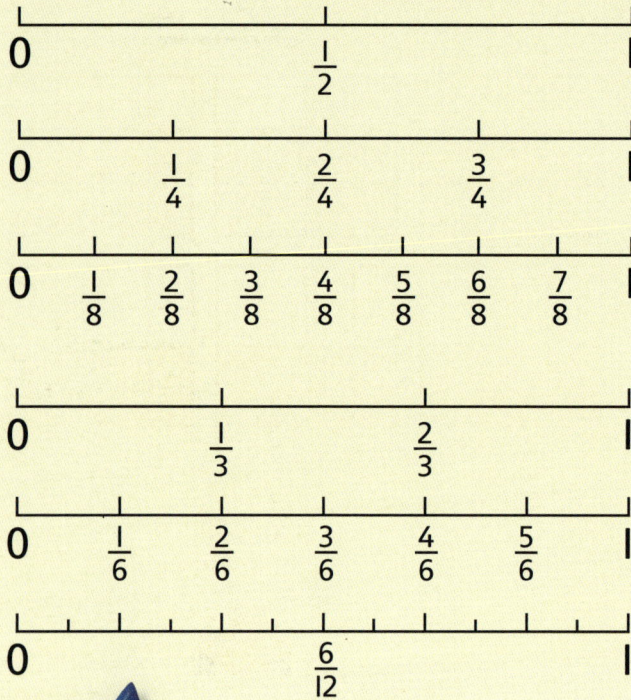

$0 \quad \frac{1}{2} \quad |$

$0 \quad \frac{1}{4} \quad \frac{2}{4} \quad \frac{3}{4} \quad |$

$0 \quad \frac{1}{8} \quad \frac{2}{8} \quad \frac{3}{8} \quad \frac{4}{8} \quad \frac{5}{8} \quad \frac{6}{8} \quad \frac{7}{8} \quad |$

$0 \quad \frac{1}{3} \quad \frac{2}{3} \quad |$

$0 \quad \frac{1}{6} \quad \frac{2}{6} \quad \frac{3}{6} \quad \frac{4}{6} \quad \frac{5}{6} \quad |$

$0 \quad \frac{6}{12} \quad |$

1. $\frac{1}{4} = \frac{2}{8}$

1 $\quad \frac{1}{4} = \frac{\square}{8}$

2 $\quad \frac{1}{2} = \frac{\square}{4}$

3 $\quad \frac{4}{8} = \frac{\square}{4}$

4 $\quad \frac{3}{4} = \frac{\square}{8}$

5 $\quad \frac{1}{2} = \frac{\square}{8}$

6 $\quad \frac{1}{3} = \frac{\square}{6}$

7 $\quad \frac{3}{6} = \frac{\square}{12}$

8 $\quad \frac{1}{6} = \frac{\square}{12}$

9 $\quad \frac{2}{3} = \frac{\square}{12}$

10 $\quad \frac{4}{6} = \frac{\square}{3}$

11 $\quad \frac{5}{6} = \frac{\square}{12}$

Use these lines to write some pairs of equivalent fractions:

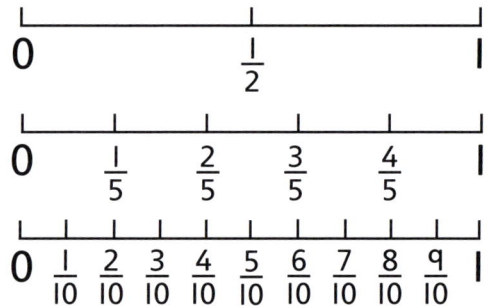

$0 \quad \frac{1}{2} \quad |$

$0 \quad \frac{1}{5} \quad \frac{2}{5} \quad \frac{3}{5} \quad \frac{4}{5} \quad |$

$0 \quad \frac{1}{10} \quad \frac{2}{10} \quad \frac{3}{10} \quad \frac{4}{10} \quad \frac{5}{10} \quad \frac{6}{10} \quad \frac{7}{10} \quad \frac{8}{10} \quad \frac{9}{10} \quad |$

12 Write pairs of letters for the equivalent fractions.

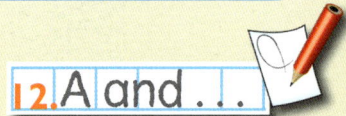

12. A and . . .

A	B	C	D	E	F	G
$\frac{2}{6}$	$\frac{3}{5}$	$\frac{3}{4}$	$\frac{1}{2}$	$\frac{2}{10}$	$\frac{1}{4}$	$\frac{1}{3}$

H	I	J	K	L	M	N
$\frac{2}{3}$	$\frac{6}{8}$	$\frac{1}{5}$	$\frac{2}{4}$	$\frac{4}{6}$	$\frac{2}{8}$	$\frac{6}{10}$

13 Write another equivalent fraction for each pair.

I can find fractions that are equal

Fractions in their simplest form

What are the factors of these numbers?

1 20   **2** 30   **3** 16   **4** 28

5 12   **6** 8   **7** 18   **8** 32

9 25   **10** 36   **11** 24   **12** 40

Write these fractions in their simplest form:

$$13. \frac{2}{4} = \frac{1}{2}$$

13 $\frac{2}{4}$ **14** $\frac{2}{8}$ **15** $\frac{6}{9}$ **16** $\frac{3}{12}$

17 $\frac{2}{10}$ **18** $\frac{10}{15}$ **19** $\frac{6}{8}$ **20** $\frac{12}{20}$

21 $\frac{8}{12}$ **22** $\frac{12}{30}$ **23** $\frac{32}{40}$ **24** $\frac{6}{36}$

Use numbers 0–100 to make a fraction that can be simplified.

Write all the simpler fractions that you can make.

Beside each fraction write the factor(s) you used.

Show the simplest fraction.

Original fraction	Factors	Simpler fraction
$\frac{64}{80}$	2	$\frac{32}{40}$
$\frac{64}{80}$	4	$\frac{16}{20}$
$\frac{64}{80}$	8	$\frac{8}{10}$
$\frac{64}{80}$	16	$\frac{4}{5}$ is the simplest fraction

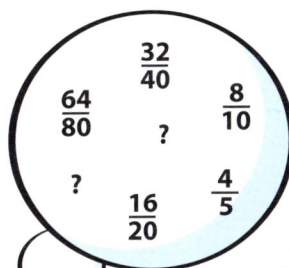

$\frac{32}{40}$ $\frac{64}{80}$? $\frac{8}{10}$? $\frac{16}{20}$ $\frac{4}{5}$

I can work out the simplest form of a fraction

Fractions in their simplest form

Write these fractions in their simplest form.

$$1. \frac{9}{12} = \frac{3}{4}$$

1. $\frac{9}{12}$
2. $\frac{8}{10}$
3. $\frac{6}{9}$
4. $\frac{12}{18}$

5. $\frac{15}{40}$
6. $\frac{20}{24}$
7. $\frac{18}{30}$
8. $\frac{21}{28}$

9. $\frac{14}{42}$
10. $\frac{36}{100}$
11. $\frac{24}{50}$
12. $\frac{49}{63}$

Copy and complete.

13. $\frac{\square}{5} = \frac{6}{10}$

14. $\frac{4}{7} = \frac{\square}{21}$

15. $\frac{5}{\square} = \frac{20}{36}$

16. $\frac{2}{3} = \frac{16}{\square}$

17. $\frac{15}{40} = \frac{\square}{8}$

18. $\frac{\square}{42} = \frac{5}{6}$

19. $\frac{1}{9} = \frac{8}{\square}$

20. $\frac{7}{\square} = \frac{28}{20}$

21. $\frac{\square}{3} = \frac{28}{21}$

22. $\frac{21}{\square} = \frac{3}{4}$

23. $\frac{25}{45} = \frac{5}{\square}$

24. $\frac{7}{8} = \frac{\square}{48}$

Create some pairs of equivalent fractions that have a missing number. Challenge your partner to solve them.

I can work out the simplest form of a fraction

Fractions in their simplest form

Write these fractions in their simplest form:

$$1. \frac{5}{10} = \frac{1}{2}$$

1 $\frac{5}{10}$ **2** $\frac{2}{8}$ **3** $\frac{6}{12}$ **4** $\frac{4}{6}$

5 $\frac{6}{10}$ **6** $\frac{8}{12}$ **7** $\frac{10}{15}$ **8** $\frac{8}{10}$

For each fraction, create two other fractions which are equivalent.

9 $\frac{6}{12}$ **10** $\frac{8}{10}$ **11** $\frac{9}{12}$ **12** $\frac{1}{2}$

Circle any fractions which are in the simplest form.

Burt is 80 today. His cake has 80 candles but he only blew out 60. What fraction of the candles did he blow out? What is that fraction in its simplest form?

How many steps did you take to make this fraction into its simplest form? Could you have taken fewer steps?

On her 80th birthday Edith blew out 72 of her candles. Can you write this as a fraction in its simplest form?

Create some fractions with large numerators and denominators for your partner to write in the simplest form. Challenge them to take as few steps as possible.

Fractions in their simplest form

Simplify each fraction and turn it into a mixed number.

$$1. \frac{9}{6} = \frac{3}{2} = 1\frac{1}{2}$$

1 $\dfrac{9}{6}$ 2 $\dfrac{14}{10}$ 3 $\dfrac{18}{4}$ 4 $\dfrac{34}{8}$

5 $\dfrac{26}{8}$ 6 $\dfrac{14}{10}$ 7 $\dfrac{42}{4}$ 8 $\dfrac{40}{6}$

Use = or ≠ to make true statements.

$$9. \frac{18}{8} \neq \frac{21}{4}$$

9 $\dfrac{18}{8}$ ☐ $\dfrac{21}{4}$ 10 $\dfrac{32}{3}$ ☐ $\dfrac{96}{9}$ 11 $\dfrac{26}{7}$ ☐ $\dfrac{104}{28}$

12 $\dfrac{24}{5}$ ☐ $\dfrac{26}{10}$ 13 $\dfrac{22}{5}$ ☐ $\dfrac{66}{15}$ 14 $\dfrac{45}{12}$ ☐ $\dfrac{25}{6}$

15 Make up three examples like this for your partner to solve.

Hughie wrote an improper fraction then simplified it to get $1\frac{1}{2}$.

What fractions might he have written?

I can use my knowledge of mixed numbers and improper fractions to help me simplify fractions

Ordering Fractions

Write each pair of fractions, smallest first.

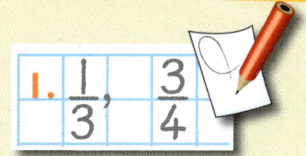

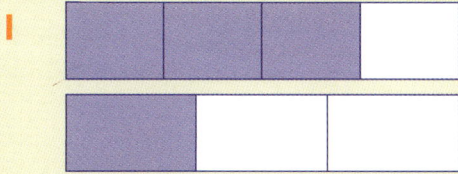

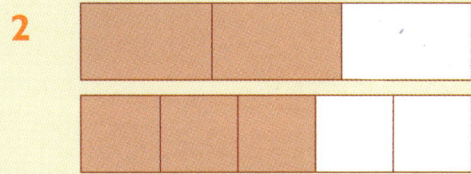

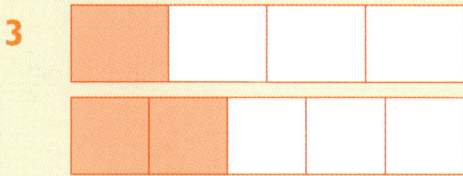

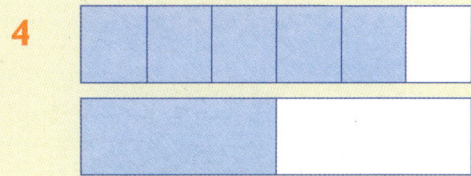

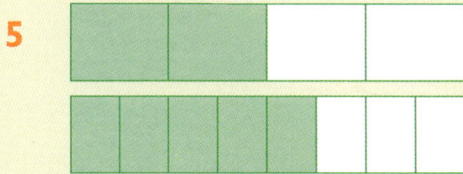

1

2

3

4

5

6

Write the three fractions in order, smallest first.

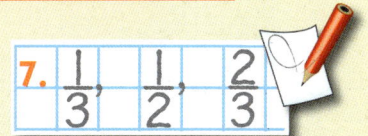

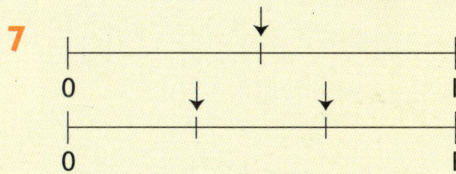

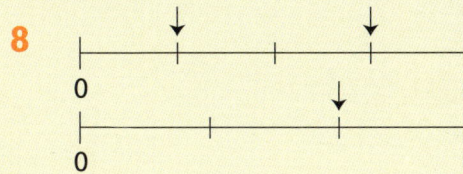

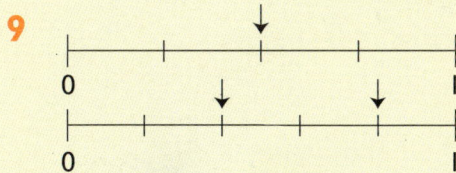

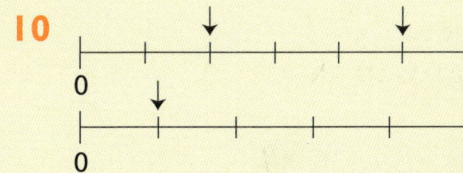

7

8

9

10

For questions 7-10 write the fractions so they have the same denominator, to show that your order is correct.

I can compare and order fractions

Ordering Fractions

1 Write the fraction. Then simplify it if you can.

$$\text{1. a: } \frac{6}{12} = \frac{1}{2}$$

h   f   b   d   a   e   f   c   g

0   1

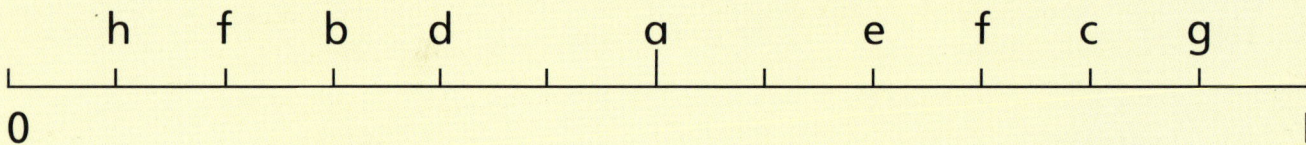

Write < or > between each pair of fractions.

2 $\frac{5}{8}$, $\frac{1}{2}$

3 $\frac{6}{15}$, $\frac{1}{3}$

4 $\frac{4}{5}$, $\frac{18}{20}$

5 $\frac{1}{2}$, $\frac{7}{16}$

6 $\frac{3}{8}$, $\frac{1}{4}$

7 $\frac{7}{15}$, $\frac{13}{30}$

Draw a number line with 16 sections. Number the ends 0 and 1.
Mark these fractions on it:

8 $\frac{1}{16}$

9 $\frac{1}{2}$

10 $\frac{3}{8}$

11 $\frac{3}{4}$

12 $\frac{7}{8}$

13 $\frac{15}{16}$

14 $\frac{1}{4}$

15 $\frac{5}{8}$

You need a 0–1 line marked in 10ths and a 0–1 line marked in 12ths.

You and your partner each have one of the lines. Each choose a position on your line and say the fraction there. Work out which fraction is larger.

Write them out, putting > or < or = between them. Do this again, several times.

I can compare and order fractions

Ordering Fractions

Write each set of fractions in order, smallest first. Draw your own fraction lines to help you.

1   $\frac{5}{6}$, $\frac{5}{12}$

2   $\frac{2}{3}$, $\frac{3}{5}$

3   $\frac{5}{6}$, $\frac{7}{8}$

4   $\frac{5}{12}$, $\frac{5}{6}$, $\frac{3}{4}$

5   $\frac{7}{15}$, $\frac{1}{2}$, $\frac{4}{5}$

6   $\frac{1}{7}$, $\frac{2}{3}$, $\frac{2}{21}$

7   $\frac{4}{9}$, $\frac{5}{18}$, $\frac{1}{2}$

8   $\frac{7}{10}$, $\frac{3}{5}$, $\frac{1}{2}$

9   $\frac{7}{12}$, $\frac{19}{24}$, $\frac{5}{6}$

10   $\frac{17}{30}$, $\frac{4}{5}$, $\frac{1}{3}$

11   $\frac{15}{24}$, $\frac{3}{8}$, $\frac{2}{3}$

12   $\frac{1}{5}$, $\frac{27}{30}$, $\frac{5}{6}$

Cho has 12 marbles. She shares them between three friends, giving $\frac{1}{2}$ to one friend, $\frac{1}{6}$ to another and $\frac{1}{3}$ to the other. What other fractions could she use to share the marbles?

True or false?

13   Ten thirtieths is double one sixth.

14   $\frac{2}{7}$ is half of $\frac{20}{35}$

15   One half is one fifth more than three tenths.

16   $\frac{16}{40} = \frac{3}{5}$

17   Double one fifth is half of eight tenths.

18   One half of ten sixtieths is half of one twelfth.

I can compare and order fractions

Fractions of amounts

Write the fractions of the page of stamps.

Hint: Use the lines to help you.

1. $\frac{1}{2}$ of 8 = 4

1

$\frac{1}{2}$ of 8 = ☐ $\frac{1}{4}$ of 8 = ☐

2

$\frac{1}{2}$ of 12 = ☐ $\frac{1}{3}$ of 12 = ☐ $\frac{1}{6}$ of 12 = ☐

3

$\frac{1}{2}$ of 10 = ☐ $\frac{1}{5}$ of 10 = ☐

4

$\frac{1}{2}$ of 18 = ☐ $\frac{1}{3}$ of 18 = ☐ $\frac{1}{6}$ of 18 = ☐

Complete the fractions of the coins.

Hint: Use 1p coins to help you.

5

$\frac{1}{3}$ of ☐ p = ☐ p

6

$\frac{1}{4}$ of ☐ p = ☐ p

7 $\frac{1}{2}$ of 10p = ☐ p   **8** $\frac{1}{4}$ of 20p = ☐ p   **9** $\frac{1}{3}$ of 12p = ☐ p

10 $\frac{1}{5}$ of 15p = ☐ p   **11** $\frac{1}{2}$ of 14p = ☐ p   **12** $\frac{1}{4}$ of 16p = ☐ p

How many 1p coins do you need to be able to split the same set into halves, thirds, quarters and fifths?

I can find unit fractions of amounts

Fractions of amounts

1   In a class of 32, $\frac{1}{4}$ are absent. Of those present, $\frac{1}{3}$ are boys. How many girls are present?

2   Snappy the crocodile was born with 40 teeth. He lost $\frac{1}{5}$ of his teeth in his first year, and another $\frac{1}{4}$ of those left in the next year. How many teeth does he have left now?

3   Sarita bought a tin of 60 fruit gums. She kept $\frac{1}{3}$ for herself, gave $\frac{1}{4}$ to her sister and $\frac{1}{5}$ to her brother. How many are left for her mum and dad?

Choose a number between 15 and 25. Take that many counters.

Find different fractions of that number and write them down.

$\frac{1}{4}$ of 20 = 5

$\frac{1}{3}$ of 21 = 7

Write the difference between:

4   $\frac{1}{4}$ of 12 and $\frac{1}{3}$ of 15

5   $\frac{1}{7}$ of 42 and $\frac{1}{4}$ of 36

6   $\frac{1}{5}$ of 45 and $\frac{1}{4}$ of 40

7   $\frac{1}{10}$ of 90 and $\frac{1}{8}$ of 56

8   $\frac{1}{6}$ of 72 and $\frac{1}{3}$ of 54

9   $\frac{1}{5}$ of 100 and $\frac{1}{4}$ of 100

Make up another problem, like the questions you have just done. Aim for a difference of 5. Find several solutions if you can.

I can solve problems about finding unit fractions of amounts

Fractions of amounts

For each pair of grids, write the coloured fractions.

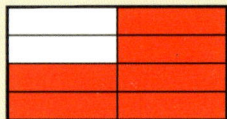

1. $\frac{1}{4}$ of 8 = 2

 $\frac{3}{4}$ of 8 = 6

1

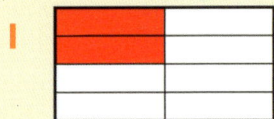

$\frac{1}{4}$ of 8 =

$\frac{3}{4}$ of 8 =

2
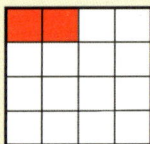 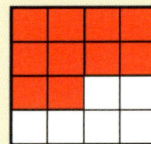

$\frac{1}{3}$ of 6 = $\frac{2}{3}$ of 6 =

3
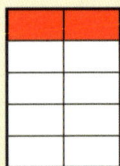 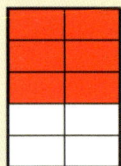

$\frac{1}{5}$ of 10 = $\frac{3}{5}$ of 10 =

4
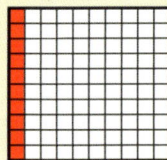 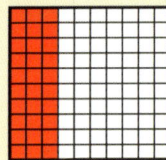

$\frac{1}{8}$ of 16 = $\frac{5}{8}$ of 16 =

5
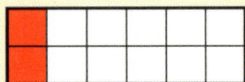 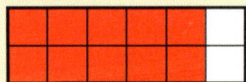

$\frac{1}{6}$ of 12 = $\frac{5}{6}$ of 12 =

6

$\frac{1}{10}$ of 100 = $\frac{3}{10}$ of 100 =

Copy and complete.

7 $\frac{1}{10}$ of £70 = $\frac{3}{10}$ of £70 =

8 $\frac{1}{5}$ of 15 cm = $\frac{2}{5}$ of 15 cm =

9 $\frac{1}{4}$ of 32 kg = $\frac{3}{4}$ of 32 kg =

10 $\frac{1}{8}$ of 40 ml = $\frac{7}{8}$ of 40 ml =

Investigate some different amounts, less than £100, that you can find $\frac{3}{5}$ of.

I can find unit fractions of amounts

Fractions of amounts

Copy and complete.

1 $\frac{1}{3}$ of 9 = ☐   ⟶ $\frac{2}{3}$ of 9 = ☐

2 $\frac{1}{4}$ of 12 = ☐   ⟶ $\frac{3}{4}$ of 12 = ☐

3 $\frac{1}{5}$ of 20 = ☐   ⟶ $\frac{4}{5}$ of 20 = ☐

4 $\frac{1}{6}$ of 42 = ☐   ⟶ $\frac{5}{6}$ of 42 = ☐

5 $\frac{1}{10}$ of 60 = ☐   ⟶ $\frac{7}{10}$ of 60 = ☐

6 $\frac{1}{8}$ of 64 = ☐   ⟶ $\frac{3}{8}$ of 64 = ☐

7 $\frac{3}{5}$ of 15 = ☐   8 $\frac{3}{4}$ of 28 = ☐   9 $\frac{7}{10}$ of 80 = ☐

I am a number. Who am I?

10 I am one half of a fifth of 20.

11 I am 3 less than double one third of 21.

12 I am 5 more than a fifth of double 20.

13 I am half the total of one sixth of 24 and one third of 18.

14 I am the difference between one quarter of 60 and one fifth of 60.

15 I am the total of one half, one third and one quarter of 24.

Invent your own 'Who am I?' problems using fractions, with the answers. Try them on a friend.

I can find unit fractions of numbers and use them to find other fractions

Finding fractions of amounts

Write how much each child has saved.

1. $\frac{1}{4}$ of £48 = £12	
$\frac{3}{4}$ of £48 =	

1 Target £48

saved $\frac{3}{4}$

2 Target £27

saved $\frac{2}{3}$

3 Target £45

saved $\frac{2}{5}$

4 Target £60

saved $\frac{3}{10}$

5 Target £30

saved $\frac{4}{5}$

6 Target £24

saved $\frac{3}{8}$

7 Target £30

saved $\frac{5}{6}$

8 Target £28

saved $\frac{4}{7}$

9 Target £45

saved $\frac{7}{9}$

You need £60 to reach your target. What fraction could you have saved, and what could your target be? For example, you could have saved $\frac{1}{2}$ of a target of £120.

Copy and complete.

10. $\frac{1}{5}$ of £25 = £5, $\frac{3}{5}$ of £25 = £15

10 $\frac{3}{5}$ of £25 =

11 $\frac{2}{3}$ of 21 cm =

12 $\frac{7}{10}$ of 80 g =

13 $\frac{3}{4}$ of 12 km =

14 $\frac{5}{6}$ of 300 ml =

15 $\frac{7}{9}$ of 18 m =

16 $\frac{3}{8}$ of 40 l =

17 $\frac{2}{7}$ of 63 kg =

18 $\frac{4}{6}$ of 18 g =

19 $\frac{2}{3}$ of 24 cm =

20 $\frac{5}{7}$ of 63 l =

21 $\frac{3}{4}$ of 48 m =

I can find unit fractions of amounts and use them to find other fractions

Tenths

Write each as a fraction.

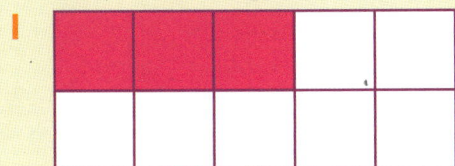

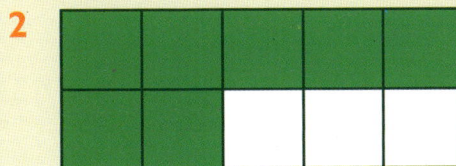

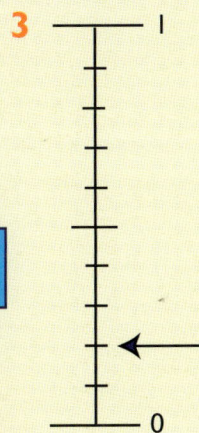

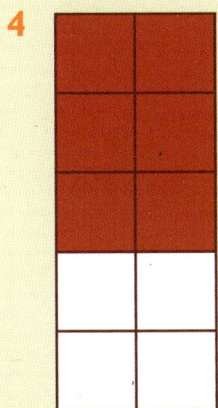

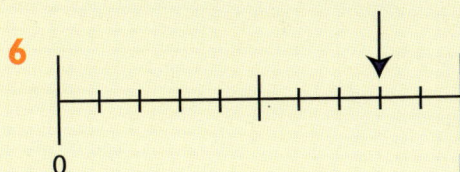

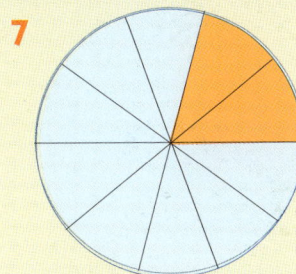

1. $\dfrac{3}{10}$

1

2

3

4

5

6

7

Write each as a decimal.

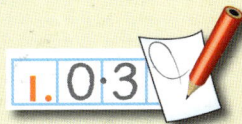

1. 0.3

Write these in order, smallest to largest.

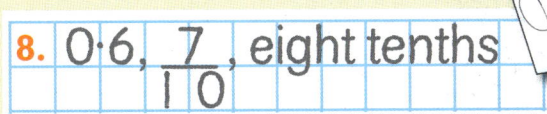

8. 0.6, $\dfrac{7}{10}$, eight tenths

8 0.6, eight tenths, $\dfrac{7}{10}$

9 four tenths, 0.3, $\dfrac{5}{10}$

10 seven tenths, 0.9, $\dfrac{8}{10}$

11 0.7, $\dfrac{3}{10}$, 0.5

12 $\dfrac{5}{10}$, $\dfrac{8}{10}$, 0.6

13 $\dfrac{3}{10}$, $\dfrac{1}{2}$, 0.4

Write your own set of fractions and decimals.
Swap with your partner and put them in order.

I can change a tenths fraction to a decimal

Tenths

This is one whole.
Write each collection as a mixed number.

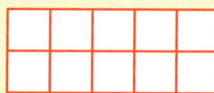

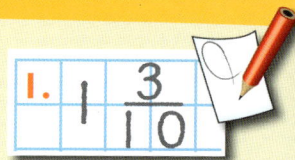

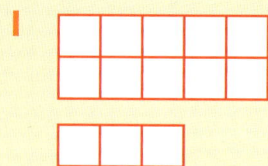

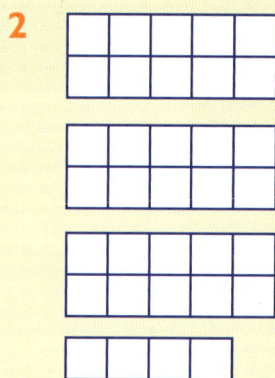

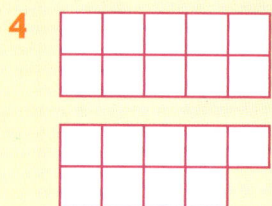

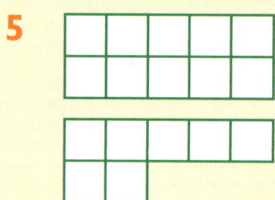

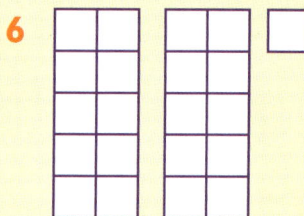

1. $1\frac{3}{10}$

1

2

3

4

5

6

Write each as a decimal.

1. $1 \cdot 3$

Write each number as a tenths fraction.

7. $1\frac{3}{10}$

7 $1\frac{3}{10}$

8 $2\frac{1}{10}$

9 $3\frac{6}{10}$

10 $4\frac{4}{10}$

11 $11\frac{7}{10}$

12 $3\frac{1}{2}$

13 $1\cdot7$

14 $2\cdot3$

Look at your answers to questions 7 to 14. Write the fractions in order, smallest to largest. Choose two of them that are next-door numbers. Ask your partner to write a number in between.

I can change a tenths fraction to a decimal

Tenths

I   Write the position of these pointers.

d   g   c   a   h   e   b   f

0   I   2   3   4

Collect 10 tokens for a free tub of ice-cream. Write how many tubs you can have with these tokens.

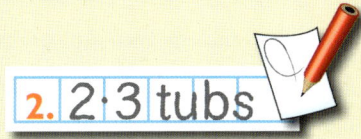

2. 2·3 tubs

| 2 | 23 tokens | 3 | 47 tokens | 4 | 16 tokens |
| 5 | 38 tokens | 6 | 54 tokens | 7 | 79 tokens |

How many more tokens would you need to get a complete number of tubs each time?

Use one of each of these cards: 3 7 2 5

Make different decimal numbers like this:

How many can you make between 3·3 and 7·3?
How many can you make that are not between these numbers?
Write them all out in order, smallest first.

Hundredths

Write the amount in each pile.

1. £6·59

1

2

3

4

5

6

7 Write the amounts in order, smallest to largest.

Write the letter to match each of these positions on the lines:

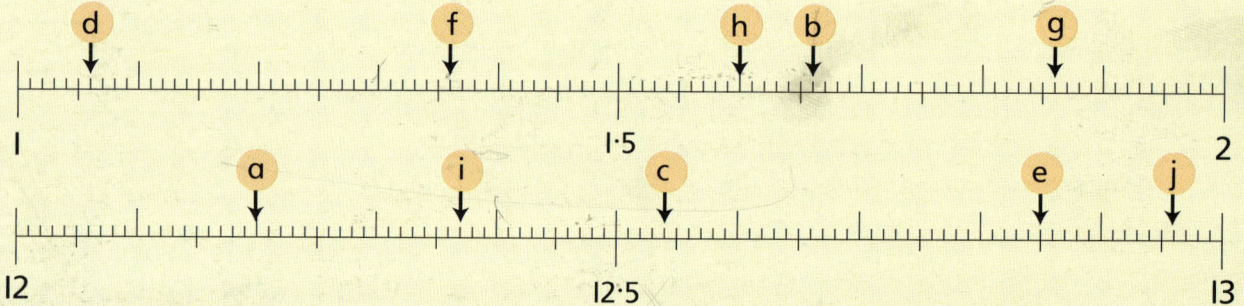

| **8** 1·66 | **9** 12·2 | **10** 1·36 | **11** 12·54 | **12** 1·6 |
| **13** 12·85 | **14** 1·06 | **15** 12·96 | **16** 1·86 | **17** 12·37 |

How many numbers with two decimal places are there between 1·5 and 2·12 that have 1 as their hundredths digit? 2 as their hundredths digit?

I can identify the position of a number with two decimal places on a number line

Tenths and hundredths

What fraction of the square is dark green? Write it as tenths and hundredths.

$$1. \frac{3\,5}{100} = 0.35$$

1

2

3

4

5

6

$\frac{1}{4} = 25$ hundredths. Explore other fractions that can be written as hundredths.

Copy and complete.

$$7. 37 \text{ hundredths} = \frac{3}{10} + \frac{7}{100}$$

7 37 hundredths = $\frac{\square}{10} + \frac{7}{100}$

8 $\frac{46}{100} = \square$ tenths + $\square$ hundredths

9 $2\frac{64}{100} = 2 + \frac{\square}{10} + \frac{\square}{100}$

10 74 hundredths = $\frac{\square}{10} + \frac{\square}{100}$

11 $4\frac{32}{100} = 4 + \frac{\square}{10} + \frac{\square}{100}$

I can talk about how many hundredths are in a tenth

Tenths and hundredths

Copy and complete.

1   80 hundredths = ☐ tenths

2   17 tenths = ☐ hundredths

3   320 hundredths = ☐ tenths

4   100 tenths = ☐ hundredths

Write the value of the highlighted digit.

1.4 units

5   **4**·32

6   5·1**6**

7   7·**8**

8   2·0**4**

9   **1**7·38

10   26·**4**1

11   8·**3**0

12   **3**4·17

13   2·3**9**

14   ☐·☐☐

15   2**7**

16   0·0**6**

17   6·4**2**

18   9**3**

19   1**2**·7

20   7·0**6**

True or false?

21   0·6 = 0·60

22   0·73 = 0·7 + 0·03

23   0·64 > 0·8

24   0·5 < 0·37

25   $2\frac{37}{100} < 2\cdot4$

26   $1\cdot6 > 1\frac{57}{100}$

Copy and complete.

27   3·58 = 3 units + ☐ tenths + 8 hundredths

28   4·69 = 4 units + ☐ tenths + ☐ hundredths

29   7·56 = ☐ units + 5 ☐ + 6 ☐

What happens when you split up 3·07 or 3·7 in this way?

I can talk about how many hundredths are in a tenth

Ordering decimals

Name	Running time (s)	Swimming time (s)	Cycling time (s)
Sufia	12·34	39·48	27·4
Chang	12·4	40·25	27·03
Emma	12·37	39·9	28·2
Josh	12·45	40·1	28·05
Vijay	12·03	40·06	27·2
Scott	12·33	39·55	28·47
Kim	12·35	40·03	27·53

1. Running: Vijay
Swimming: Sufia
Cycling: Chang

In each race, who:

1 won?

2 came third?

3 came fifth?

4 came last?

5 came just after Emma?

6 came just before Josh?

7 What is the time difference between the first and last in each race?

8 In the three races, who had the shortest overall time?

Write a number between:

9 5·6 and 6·5

10 4·32 and 4·35

11 4·7 and 4·8

12 4·65 and 4·6

13 4·7 and 4·72

14 5 and 4·96

Use one of each of these digit cards: 4 7 0 6

Make decimal numbers, either ☐.☐ or ☐.☐☐.

Investigate how many numbers you can make between 5 and 8. Put them in order.

Rounding

Write the position of each pointer.
Round it to the nearest whole number.

1. a: 4·2 → 4

1

a   c   d   b

4   5

2

g   h   e   f

10   11

3

j   k   i

0   1

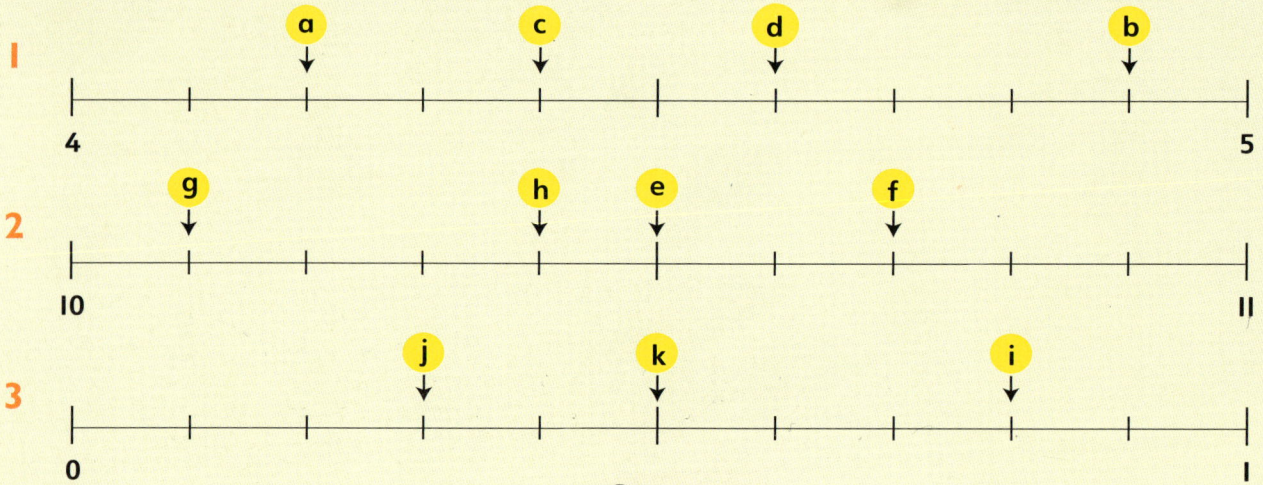

Round the weight of each cat to the nearest kilogram.

Cat SHOW

4. 6·3 kg → 6 kg

4 6·3 kg

5 8·4 kg

6 4·9 kg

7 7·2 kg

8 2·3 kg

9 6·6 kg

10 5·5 kg

11 11·7 kg

12 8·8 kg

Two cats are weighed together. Their total weight when rounded is 12 kg. Which of the cats above could it be?

I can round numbers with one decimal place to the nearest whole number

Rounding

6·2 cm

4·5 cm

4·9 cm

10·7 cm

3·2 cm

4·6 cm

6·5 cm

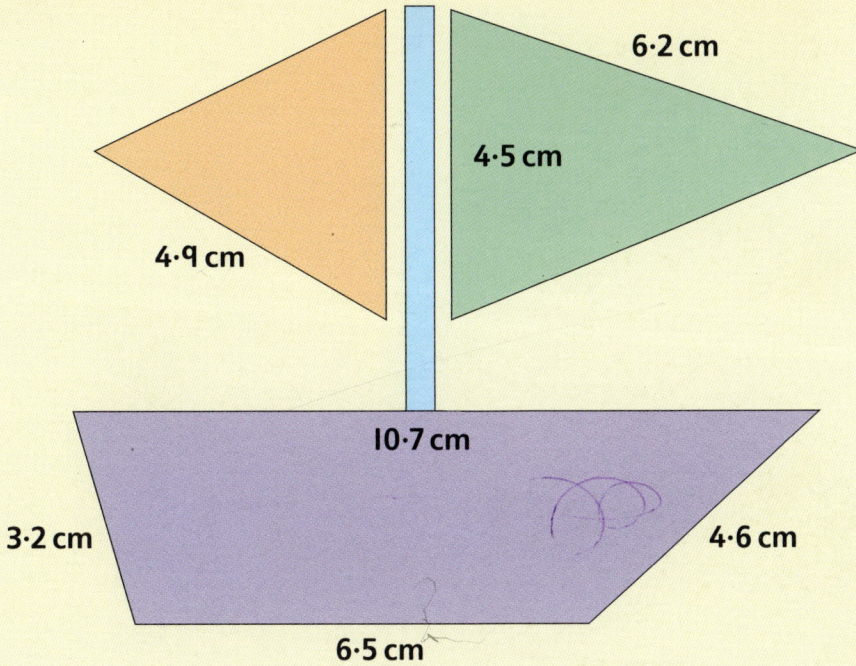

1 Round each length to the nearest centimetre.

1. 6·2 cm → 6 cm

Draw your own picture with straight lines. Measure the length of each line and round them to the nearest centimetre.

2 Write the position of each pointer. Round it to the nearest whole number.

2. a·2·62 → 3

d   b   e   a   c

2   3

g   i   j   f   h

6   7

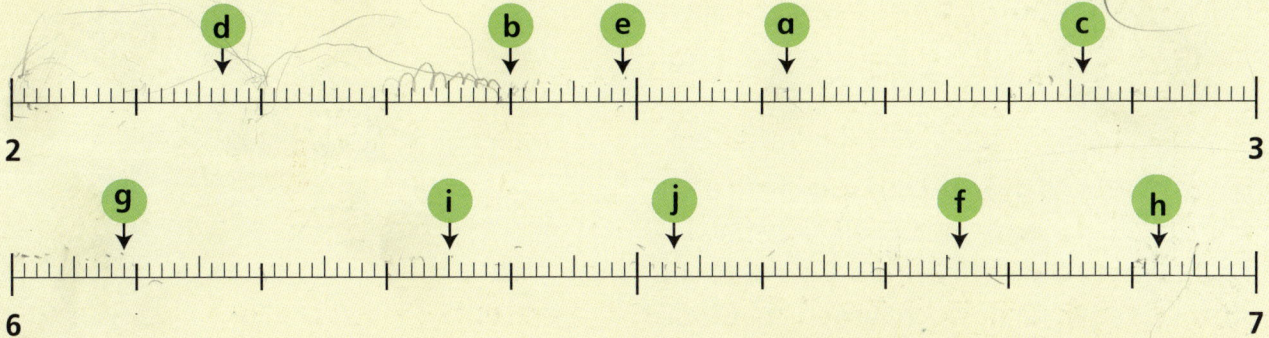

I can round a number with two decimal places to the nearest whole number

33

Rounding

Write each amount and round it to the nearest pound.

1. £4·76 → £5

1
2
3

4
5
6

7	£7·09	8	£5·97	9	£60·10	10	£4·50
11	£0·82	12	£1·04	13	£2·22	14	£0·34

You have one of each of these:

Here is an amount that rounds to £4:

Here is an amount that rounds to £11:

Investigate ways of making amounts that round to each of £1, £2, …, £20.
Using just four coins, can you still make amounts that round to each of £1, £2, …, £20?

I can round sums of money to the nearest pound

Rounding

Write the position of each pointer, then round the number to the nearest whole number, and also to the nearest tenth.

1. a: 4·42 → 4
   4·42 → 4·4

1

2

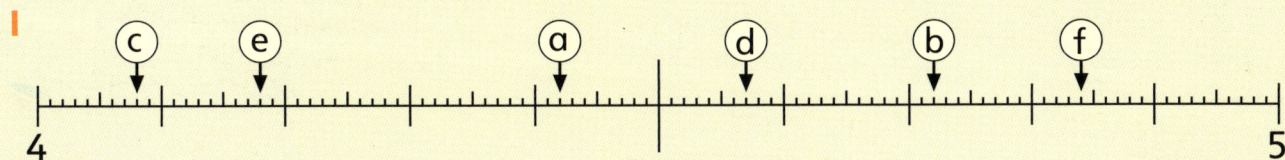

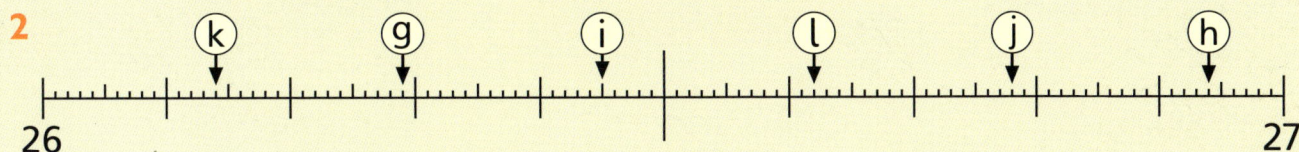

These are the distances thrown in a 'welly wanging' competition. Round each distance to the nearest metre and also to the nearest tenth of a metre.

3. 34·62 → 35 m
   34·62 → 34·6 m

3   34·62 m

4   18·49 m

5   13·27 m

6   25·34 m

7   11·08 m

8   19·46 m

If Jemma's welly throw rounded to the nearest whole metre was 24 m and Ricky's was 18 m, investigate the smallest and largest possible real difference between their distances.

Rounding

These are the prices for train tickets. Round each price to the nearest
a: pound and b: 10p.

1. £8·38 → a: £8   b: £8·40

1	Bodlington £8·38	2	Tarfield £14·52	3	Brookby £26·35
4	Dormouth £9·18	5	Jerby £32·41	6	Bottingham £18·76
7	Duxton £48·48	8	Backfield £32·91	9	Yutton £16·85
10	Wellstone £25·36	11	Bradby £17·18	12	Downscombe £42·67

If Su Li buys these two tickets, find the total cost, then round
it to the nearest pound and 10p.

13 Jerby and Brookby

14 Tarfield and Backfield

15 Bodlington and Yutton

16 Bradby and Dormouth

17 Duxton and Wellstone

18 Downscombe and Bradby

19 Bottingham and Dormouth

20 Brookby and Backfield

21 Dormouth and Jerby

Are the answers the same if Su Li rounds both prices to the nearest pound first, then adds the two rounded amounts?

I can round sums of money to the nearest pound and to the nearest 10p

Rounding

Tim  Kim
12·37 s   15·64 s

Kat  Pat
15·14 s   12·88 s

Ben  Den
13·36 s   14·49 s

Sam  Pam
11·59 s   16·32 s

Each person runs 100 m. Write the time, rounded to the nearest second, for:

1. 12·37 s → 12 s

1 Tim   **2** Sam   **3** Pat   **4** Ben   **5** Kim   **6** Den.

In the relay, the time for each pair of runners is added. Write the total times, rounded to the nearest second, for:

7 Tim and Kim   **8** Sam and Pam   **9** Ben and Den.

In the relay, who came: **10** first   **11** third   **12** last?

Ruth and Ian each have an amount of money.
To the nearest pound, Ruth has £4 and Ian has £6.
The total of Ruth and Ian's amounts does not round
to £10. What could the amounts be? Give some examples.
Can you explain why?

 I can round a number with two decimal places to the nearest whole number

Multiplying by 10, 100 and 1000

Multiply each number by 10.

$$1.\ 2{\cdot}3 = 2\ \text{units} + 3\ \text{tenths}$$
$$2{\cdot}3 \times 10 = (2\ \text{units} \times 10) + (3\ \text{tenths} \times 10)$$
$$= 20 + 3$$
$$= 23$$

1	2·3	2	4·8	3	3·6
4	3·4	5	5·7	6	8·6
7	14·2	8	12·5	9	17·6
10	20·7	11	44·8		

Create a poster which explains the rule for multiplying by 10.

Use a similar method to multiply these numbers by 100.

12	3·7	13	8·6	14	4·57	15	10·35

Multiply these numbers by 100.
Only show your working if you want to.

16	7·06	17	38·07	18	40·06	19	105·07

Write some decimal numbers. Multiply them by 1000.

I can multiply decimals by 10, 100 and 1000

Multiplying by 10, 100 and 1000

Write the wages for doing each job 10 times.

1. £5·50 × 10 = £55

1 Window cleaning £5·50

2 Hoovering £3·40

3 Car wash £10·50

4 Babysitting £6·65

5 Cat grooming £4·44

6 Chicken feeding £7·75

7 Bed making £3·29

8 Washing up £6·25

9 Cleaning £5·46

10 Walking the dog £10·33

11 Gardening £8·66

Write the wages for doing each job 100 times.

True or false?

12 One hundred multiplied by 7170 is the same as 10 × 71700.

13 Ten lots of fifty pounds and ten lots of five pence is fifty-five pounds.

14 Ten pounds and ten pence multiplied by ten is one hundred and ten pounds.

15 Multiplying any number by 10, by 10 again and by 10 again is the same as multiplying by 1000.

16 Ten times one hundred and one is the same as one hundred times eleven.

Start with £5·50. Multiply it by 10 five times. Talk with your partner about whether the total is going to be less than or more than £1 000 000. Now work it out!

Multiplying by 10, 100 and 1000

There are 100 cm in a metre. How many centimetres long are these vehicles?

1. $3·64 m = (3·64 × 100) cm$
   $= 364 cm$

1 3·64 m

2 4·8 m

3 2·08 m

4 14·07 m

5 0·86 m

6 0·24 m

Copy and complete.

7. $1306 × 1000 = 13060$

7 $13·06 × \boxed{} = 13060$

8 $20·08 × \boxed{} = 2008$

9 $203·4 × 100 = \boxed{}$

10 $345·04 × \boxed{} = 345040$

11 $\boxed{} × 195·3 = 1953$

12 $38·06 × \boxed{} = 38060$

How many amounts between £1 and £2 will multiply by 10 to give an exact number of pounds?

How many amounts between £1 and £10 will do the same?

I can multiply decimals by 10, 100 and 1000

Dividing by 10, 100 and 1000

Find the amount in pounds.

1. $507p = £(507 ÷ 100)$
   $= £5.07$

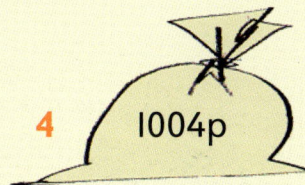

1 507p

2 643p

3 777p

4 1004p

5 990p

6 7040p

7 101p

8 2301p

9 648P

10 3709p

11 876p

12 2500p

Find some amounts that, when divided by 10 or 100, leave you with three different coins. What about four coins?

Use division to find the missing numbers.

3. $1400m = 1.4km$

13 1400 m = [ ] km

14 4780 m = [ ] km

15 3660 ml = [ ] l

16 700 ml = [ ] l

17 4880 g = [ ] kg

18 5700 m = [ ] km

19 6990 ml = [ ] l

20 4820 g = [ ] kg

21 3650 m = [ ] km

I can convert units of measurement by dividing by 10, 100 or 1000

Dividing by 10, 100 and 1000

How many 100 g weights are required to balance each object? How many extra 10 g weights are needed?

1. 4260 ÷ 100 = 42·6
   42 100g weights
   6 10g weights

1

4260 g

2

33 790 g

3

5470 g

4

2180 g

5

6190 g

6

48 210 g

7

3940 g

8

12 590 g

Write the missing numbers.

9. 3010 ÷ 1000 = 3·01

9   3010 ÷ 1000 = ☐

10   41·36 ÷ 1000 = ☐

11   38·9 ÷ ☐ = 3·89

12   ☐ ÷ 100 = 0·36

13   90·9 ÷ 1000 = ☐

14   584·2 ÷ 10 = ☐

15   ☐ ÷ 10 = 0·02

16   63·4 ÷ ☐ = 6·34

17 Tim has a huge jar containing 1040 penny coins. How much does he have in pounds? If the jar contained 1040 2p coins, how much would he have?

18 Anjilee is 1245 mm tall. Her brother Amit is 100 mm taller. How many metres tall is Amit?

19 The football ground takes £20 460 in £10 notes. How many notes is that? If the notes are bundled in groups of 10, how many bundles are there?

I can divide by 10, 100 and 1000

Percentages

Write the percentage of each grid that is coloured.

1. 60%

1	2	3	4

5	6	7	8

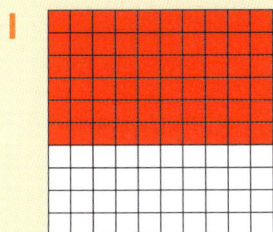

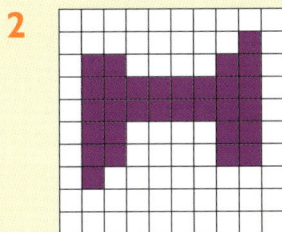

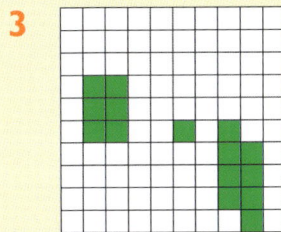

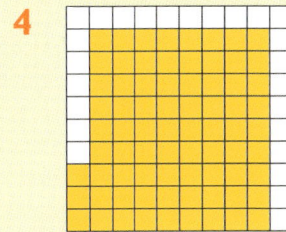

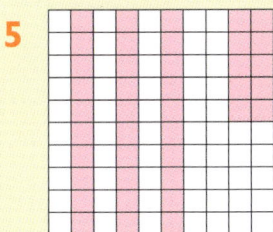

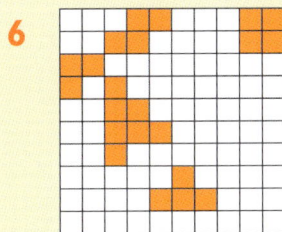

Write the percentage of each grid that is not coloured.

1. 40%

Draw a 10 × 10 grid. Colour whole squares to make your initial. You must colour at least 20% of the grid. What percentage have you coloured?

Write these fractions as percentages.

9. 80%

9 $\frac{80}{100}$ 10 $\frac{10}{100}$ 11 $\frac{45}{100}$ 12 $\frac{95}{100}$ 13 $\frac{1}{100}$

14 $\frac{1}{2}$ 15 $\frac{1}{4}$ 16 $\frac{3}{4}$ 17 $\frac{1}{5}$ 18 $\frac{7}{10}$

Write these percentages as hundredths and simplify to make another fraction.

19. $30\% = \frac{30}{100} = \frac{3}{10}$

19 30%   20 25%   21 90%   22 20%

I know that a percentage is another way to show hundredths

Percentages

How much of each square is coloured?
Write the answer as a fraction, a
decimal and a percentage.

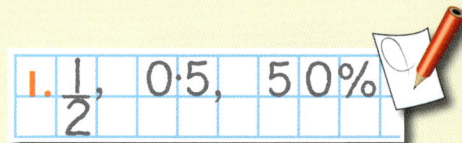

1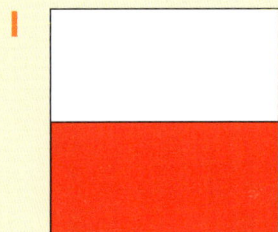

2

3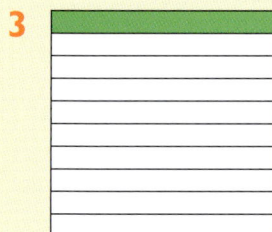

4

5

6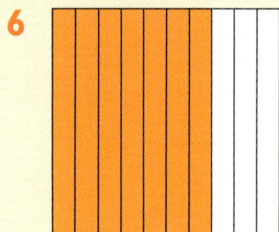

7

8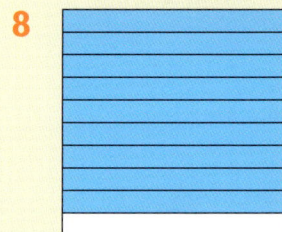

What percentage of each square is not coloured?

Draw an 8 x 10 grid.
Colour 50% of the grid red.
Colour 25% of the grid blue.
Colour 10% of the grid yellow.
How many squares are not coloured?
What percentage of the shape is not coloured?

Make up a similar challenge for your partner to do.

I can change a simple fraction into a percentage

Percentages of amounts

Write the new prices of these games in the sale.

1. £20

1 Was £40
50% off

2 Was £50
20% off

3 Was £60
10% off

4 Was £80
25% off

5 Was £100
5% off

6 Was £20
40% off

7 Was £50
60% off

8 Was £40
15% off

For the first game, what other percentage price reductions would give a whole number of pounds off?

How much is each prize worth?

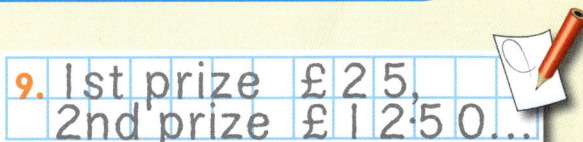
9. 1st prize £25,
2nd prize £12.50...

	Total	1st prize	2nd prize	3rd prize
9	£50	50%	25%	10%
10	£120	50%	25%	10%
11	£200	50%	25%	10%
12	£80	50%	25%	10%
13	£1000	50%	25%	10%

In each raffle, what percentage is left over? How much money is this?

9. 15%, £7.50

Percentages of amounts

Write 10% of each amount.

1. 10% of £14 = £1·40

1 £14	2 £11	3 £12	4 £5
5 £13	6 £8	7 £9	8 £15

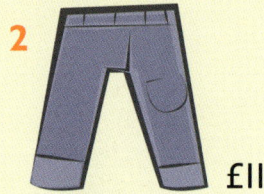

Now write 20% of each price.

Write 10% of each length as a number of centimetres.

9. 14m = 1400cm
10% of 1400cm = 140cm

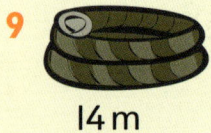

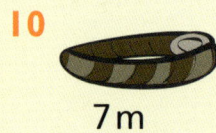

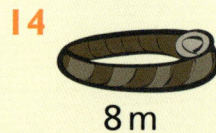

9 14 m	10 7 m	11 6 m	12 4 m
13 750 cm	14 8 m	15 3400 cm	16 22 m
17 18 m	18 230 cm	19 54 m	20 1200 cm

Is your class more or less than 10% of the school? What about other classes?

I can calculate percentages of amounts

Percentages of amounts

1 Find the matching pairs of
fractions and percentages.

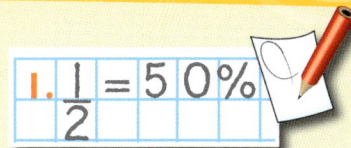

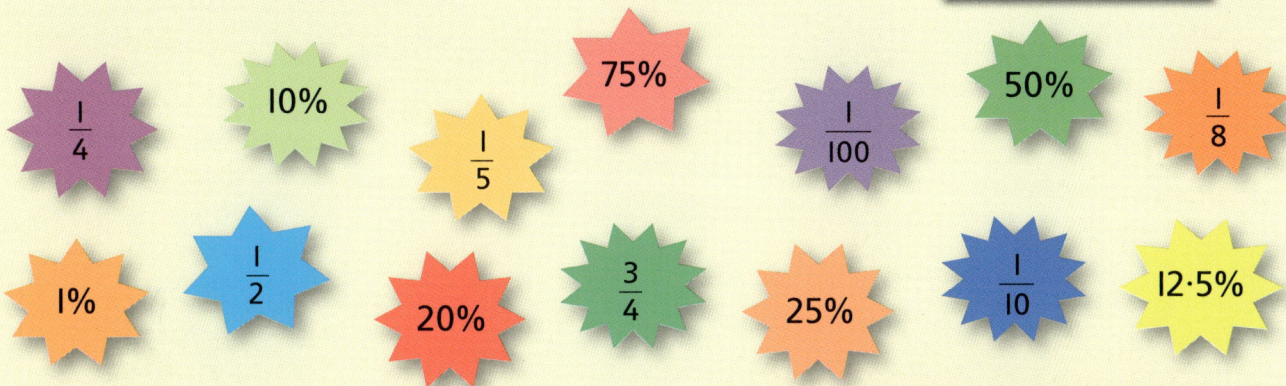

$$\frac{1}{2} = 50\%$$

$\frac{1}{4}$ 10%   75% $\frac{1}{100}$ 50% $\frac{1}{8}$

$\frac{1}{5}$

1% $\frac{1}{2}$ 20% $\frac{3}{4}$ 25% $\frac{1}{10}$ 12·5%

For each pair of items which reduction
would save you the most money?

BIG END OF SEASON REDUCTIONS

2

25% of £12   or   20% of £20

3

50% of £10   or   25% of £4

4

20% of £50   or   60% of £22

5

10% of £30   or   5% of £40

Discuss this headline.
What is wrong with it?

BIG WIN AFTER 150% EFFORT

I can calculate percentages of amounts of money

Percentages of amounts

Write the equivalent fractions in their simplest forms:

$1. \ 50\% = \frac{1}{2}$

1	50%	2	25%	3	10%	4	20%
5	70%	6	75%	7	100%	8	5%

Find 10% of the following amounts:

$9. \ 200 \div 10 = 20$
$10\% \ of \ 200 = 20$

9	200	10	360	11	580	12	240
13	1250	14	2840	15	3690	16	3570

Now calculate 30% of each amount in questions 9 to 16:

$9. \ 30\% \ of \ 200 = 3 \times 20 = 60$

Find 25% of the following amounts:

17	200	18	440	19	560	20	480
21	1640	22	2960	23	3960	24	3580

Now calculate 75% of each amount in questions 17 to 24.

A new newspaper has 40 pages.

There are 5 sections: UK news, Sport, World news, Television and Holidays.

Decide what percentage each section should have in the paper.

How many pages will there be in each section?

I can use fractions to find a percentage of an amount

Remainders

Write how many teams can be made,
and how many players are left over.

1 43 players
teams of 3

2 37 players
teams of 7

3 52 players
teams of 5

4 46 players
teams of 6

5 31 players
teams of 5

6 77 players
teams of 10

7 85 players
teams of 9

8 61 players
teams of 8

9 49 players
teams of 6

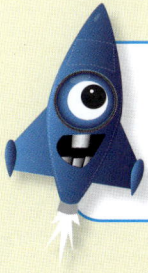

Investigate how many players you need to make teams
of 3, 4, and 5 without any remainders. What about 5, 6
and 9? Investigate some more teams like this.

Write word problems that have these answers:

10 3 r 2   **11** 4 r 1   **12** 5 r 3   **13** 6 r 4   **14** 7 r 3   **15** 2 r 1

16 3 r 7   **17** 1 r 4   **18** 3 r 7   **19** 4 r 7   **20** 3 r 6   **21** 2 r 13

I can express the answer to a division using remainders

Dividing

Complete these divisions. Write the answer using a fraction.

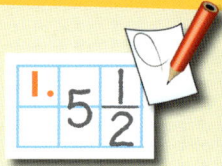

$$1. \quad 5\frac{1}{2}$$

1 $11 \div 2 =$

2 $33 \div 4 =$

3 $42 \div 5 =$

4 $23 \div 3 =$

5 $19 \div 6 =$

6 $31 \div 7 =$

7 $47 \div 10 =$

8 $29 \div 9 =$

9 $50 \div 8 =$

10 $27 \div 4 =$

11 $45 \div 6 =$

12 $85 \div 9 =$

1	2	3	4	5	6	7	8	9	10
2	4	6	8	10	12	14	16	18	20
3	6	9	12	15	18	21	24	27	30
4	8	12	16	20	24	28	32	36	40
5	10	15	20	25	30	35	40	45	50
6	12	18	24	30	36	42	48	54	60
7	14	21	28	35	42	49	56	63	70
8	16	24	32	40	48	56	64	72	80
9	18	27	36	45	54	63	72	81	90
10	20	30	40	50	60	70	80	90	100

Investigate divisions that have remainders of $\frac{1}{4}$ or $\frac{3}{4}$ in the answer.

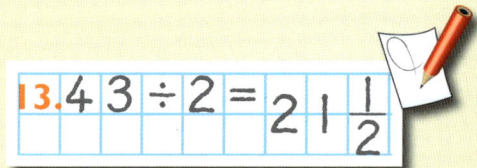

$$13. \quad 43 \div 2 = 21\frac{1}{2}$$

Krishnan's mum has made 43 flapjacks. How many would each person get if they were shared equally between:

13 2 people

14 3 people

15 4 people

16 5 people

17 6 people

18 7 people

19 8 people

20 9 people

21 10 people?

Repeat for Jed's brother, who has made 67 macaroons.

I can express the answer to a division as a fraction

Dividing

Complete the divisions, writing each answer as a decimal.

1 $31 \div 10 =$	2 $76 \div 10 =$	3 $43 \div 2 =$	4 $81 \div 2 =$
5 $17 \div 4 =$	6 $33 \div 4 =$	7 $12 \div 5 =$	8 $28 \div 5 =$
9 $28 \div 20 =$	10 $34 \div 4 =$	11 $32 \div 5 =$	12 $47 \div 5 =$

13 31 children are given an apple each. How many bags of 5 apples are needed?

14 37 racing pigeons are split into teams of 3. How many teams are there?

15 Taxis can take 4 passengers. How many taxis are needed to transport a class of 26 children and their teacher to the station?

16 Flights to Paris cost £52. How many flight tickets can be bought with £380?

17 Copy and complete the table.

	27	33	81	55	103
$\div 10$	2·7				
$\div 2$	13·5				
$\div 4$					
$\div 5$					

I can express the answer to a division as a decimal

Adding

Copy and complete.

1. $5.8 + 4.2 = 10$

```
0   1   2   3   4   5   6   7   8   9   10
```

1 $5.8 + \boxed{} = 10$ 2 $6.2 + \boxed{} = 10$ 3 $4.8 + \boxed{} = 10$

4 $5.3 + \boxed{} = 10$ 5 $6.1 + \boxed{} = 10$ 6 $\boxed{} + 9.3 = 10$

7 $\boxed{} + 3.4 = 10$ 8 $\boxed{} + 5.2 = 10$ 9 $2.7 + \boxed{} = 10$

Each rope was cut from a 10 m roll.
How much was left on the roll?

10. 5.2 m

10
4·8 m

11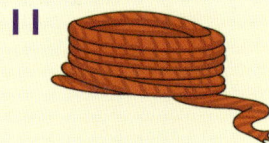
6·4 m

12
5·7 m

13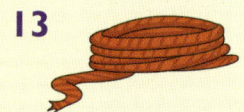
4·3 m

14
3·2 m

15
8·1 m

16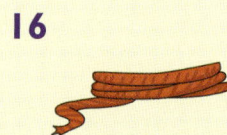
2·8 m

17
7·6 m

I have £10 in a bag. There are no notes and no coins less than 50p. There are eight coins in the bag; there are two possible combinations of coins. Find both.

I can add units and tenths to make a total of 10

Adding

How much more to make the next metre of pipe?

i. $1 \cdot 3 + 0 \cdot 7 = 2 \, m$

1 1·3 m

2 2·8 m

3 4·5 m

4 3·6 m

5 5·6 m

6 2·4 m

7 6·3 m

8 4·9 m

9 5·2 m

10 3·2 m

11 1·8 m

12 7·6 m

$\square \cdot \square + \square \cdot \square = 10$. Use digit cards 1–9.
How many ways can you find to complete this addition?

13 Choose a pair of railings to make 10 metres. Repeat five times.

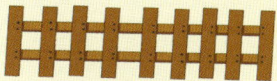
5·4 m

7·3 m

6·8 m

1·8 m

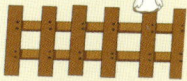
2·7 m

3·2 m

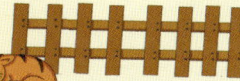
4·6 m

5·2 m

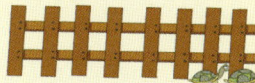
4·8 m

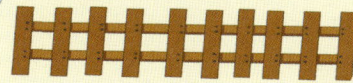
8·2 m

Copy and complete.

14 4·6 + 0·7 =

15 3·8 + 0·5 =

16 2·7 + 0·6 =

17 5·5 + 0·8 =

18 6·3 + 0·6 =

19 3·5 + 0·8 =

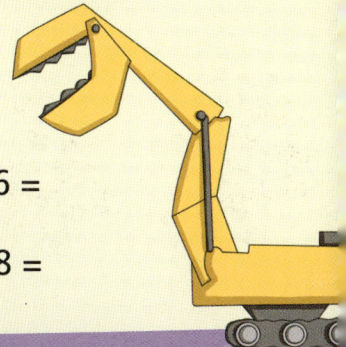

I can add units and tenths

Adding

How much more to have the next kilogram?

1. $3·6 + 0·4 = 4$ kg

1 3·6 kg	**2** 2·8 kg	**3** 5·4 kg	**4** 6·2 kg
5 4·3 kg	**6** 6·7 kg	**7** 3·1 kg	**8** 5·9 kg

Add each pair.

9. $1·2 + 1·7 = 2·9$ kg

9 1·2 kg + 1·7 kg	**10** 2·3 kg + 4·6 kg	**11** 1·6 kg + 2·8 kg
12 2·8 kg + 3·7 kg	**13** 1·8 kg + 1·5 kg	**14** 2·7 kg + 1·9 kg

15 Hervé has run 3·2 km. He reaches his friends in another 4·9 km. Then he runs home again! How far does he run?

16 Hayley cuts four pieces of rope: 1·2 m, 2·4 m, 1·8 m and 1·7 m. She ties them all together to make one long rope. The knots use 1·0 m of rope altogether. How long is her rope in the end?

17 Mrs Barker has four dogs who weigh 7·7 kg, 7·8 kg, 8·6 kg and 8·3 kg. How much do they weigh altogether?

Copy and complete.

18. $2·4 + 3·8 = 6·2$

18 2·4 + 3·8 =	**19** 3·7 + 2·4 =	**20** 6·4 + 2·8 =
21 5·3 + 2·6 =	**22** 3·6 + 5·5 =	**23** 2·5 + 2·7 =
24 4·8 + 3·6 =	**25** 2·8 + 3·9 =	**26** 7·6 + 1·5 =

I can add units and tenths

Adding

Find the answer to these sums. You might calculate like this or you might choose another method.

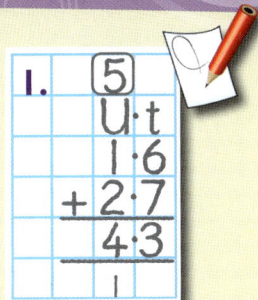

1.
```
  U · t
    5
  1 · 6
+ 2 · 7
───────
  4 · 3
    1
```

1
```
  U · t
  1 · 6
+ 2 · 7
───────
```

2
```
  U · t
  3 · 8
+ 5 · 7
───────
```

3
```
  U · t
  7 · 7
+ 9 · 5
───────
```

4
```
  U · t
  8 · 5
+ 5 · 7
───────
```

5
```
  U · t
  7 · 6
+ 6 · 5
───────
```

6
```
  U · t
  6 · 8
+ 4 · 4
───────
```

7
```
  U · t
  5 · 4
+ 6 · 7
───────
```

Dictionary
4·6 cm

Super Sums
5·8 cm

Fairy Tales
6·7 cm

Footy Facts
7·9 cm

Monster Mayhem
3·8 cm

Dinosaur Stories
5·5 cm

How much shelf space is needed for these books?

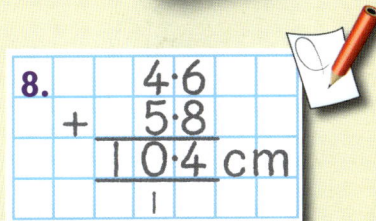

8 Dictionary and Super Sums

8.
```
    4 · 6
+   5 · 8
─────────
 1 0 · 4  cm
   1
```

9 Footy Facts and Dinosaur Stories

10 Fairy Tales and Monster Mayhem

11 Footy Facts and Super Sums

12 Which pair of books takes up the most shelf space? The least?

Find two fat books in the classroom. Measure their widths. How much shelf space do you need for them?

I can add units and tenths

Subtracting

How much has each plant grown? You might calculate like this, or you might choose another method.

1.
$$
\begin{array}{r}
1\cdot cm \\
\overset{4}{\cancel{5}}\cdot\overset{1}{2} \\
-\ 3\cdot6 \\
\hline
1\cdot6\ cm
\end{array}
$$

1
Was 3·6 cm
Now 5·2 cm

2
Was 4·7 cm
Now 6·3 cm

3
Was 3·8 cm
Now 5·4 cm

4
Was 2·7 cm
Now 6·4 cm

5
Was 4·8 cm
Now 5·2 cm

6
Was 4·6 cm
Now 7·5 cm

7
Was 5·5 cm
Now 8·3 cm

8
Was 4·3 cm
Now 6·2 cm

Choose your own methods to complete these subtractions. Show your workings.

9 5·1 − 3·7 =

10 4·4 − 3·0 =

11 7·3 − 6·7 =

12 4·7 − 1·9 =

13 6·8 − 3·4 =

14 4·0 − 3·8 =

I can do subtraction with units and tenths

Subtracting

Complete each subtraction. You might calculate like this, or you might choose another method.

1 $4\cdot3 - 2\cdot5 =$

2 $6\cdot7 - 4\cdot3 =$

3 $6\cdot5 - 1\cdot9 =$

4 $7\cdot6 - 3\cdot7 =$

5 $8\cdot6 - 3\cdot4 =$

6 $6\cdot4 - 4\cdot8 =$

7 $6\cdot3 - 1\cdot2 =$

8 $6\cdot3 - 2\cdot7 =$

9 $7\cdot2 - 4\cdot3 =$

10 $5\cdot6 - 2\cdot3 =$

$$1. \quad \begin{array}{r} 2 \\ 4\overset{3}{\cancel{}}\cdot\overset{1}{3} \\ -\ 2\cdot5 \\ \hline 1\cdot8 \end{array}$$

$\boxed{} \cdot 3 - 2 \cdot \boxed{} = 2\cdot8$. Find the missing numbers.

Frozen Lake
4·6 m

Lake Serenity
1·8 m

Lake Windrush
3·1 m

Craggy Tarn
2·6 m

Halcyon Water
3·8 m

Write the difference in the depth between the two lakes.

11 Lake Windrush and Halcyon Water

12 Lake Serenity and Halcyon Water

13 Frozen Lake and Craggy Tarn

14 Frozen Lake and Lake Windrush

15 Lake Serenity and Lake Windrush

16 Frozen Lake and Lake Serenity

17 Craggy Tarn and Halcyon Water

18 Lake Serenity and Craggy Tarn

I can do subtraction with units and tenths

Subtracting

Some water runs out of each pool. Write the number of litres left. You might calculate like this, or you might choose another method.

1.
```
      7 7
    7 ⁵
    8 6·7
  −   9·8
    7 6·9  litres
```

1

86·7 l
9.8 l runs out

2
26·5 l
8.5 l runs out

3
57·3 l
6.9 l runs out

4
62·4 l
3.7 l runs out

5
74·5 l
7.8 l runs out

6
46·3 l
9.8 l runs out

7
63·2 l
7.6 l runs out

8
55·4 l
8.6 l runs out

Look at these subtractions. Find the common mistake, then write the correct subtraction.

```
   2·7        3·1
 − 1·8      − 1·5
   1·1        2·4
```

9 Sunil goes to a football match 26·5 miles away, by bus and train. The bus journey is 2·8 miles. How far does the train travel?

10 A pipeline ran 82·3 metres from a tank to the house. If all except 17·8 m has to be replaced, how many metres is that?

11 Rover's owner buys a 6·8 kg bag of dog food. In the first week he eats 1·2 kg of food, and the week after that he eats 1·6 kg. How much is left in the bag?

I can do subtraction with units and tenths

Subtracting

Choose your own method to find the missing number.

1   9·3 – 7·1 = ☐   2   5·4 – 0·6 = ☐   3   3·2 – 1·7 = ☐

4   8·2 – ☐ = 3·8   5   9·8 – 6·7 = ☐   6   9·4 – ☐ = 4·6

7   8·7 – 5·2 = ☐   8   6·2 – 3·8 = ☐   9   3·9 – 2·7 = ☐

10   1·2 – 0·4 = ☐   11   3·6 – ☐ = 0·7   12   8·6 – ☐ = 4·9

13   7·4 – 1·3 = ☐   14   6·9 – ☐ = 6·5   15   8·6 – 4·7 = ☐

What is the difference between the two distances?

16   0·8 km   0·3 km   17   0·7 km   0·9 km

18   1·6 km   0·5 km   19   1·7 km   0·6 km

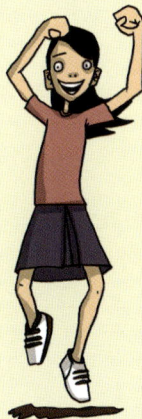

20   3·5 km   0·7 km   21   1·2 km   0·8 km

Tom and Anna ran a total of 10 km altogether. Anna ran 0·4 km further than Tom. What distance did they each run?

Adding

Find the answers to these additions.
You might calculate like this, or you might choose another method.

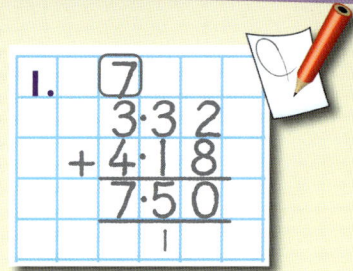

1.
$$7$$
$$3 \cdot 3\;2$$
$$+\;4 \cdot 1\;8$$
$$\overline{7 \cdot 5\;0}$$
$$1$$

1 3·32
+ 4·18
———

2 6·72
+ 3·84
———

3 4·63
+ 2·58
———

4 5·44
+ 2·83
———

5 3·67
+ 2·25
———

6 4·32
+ 3·84
———

7 6·47
+ 1·25
———

8 4·58
+ 5·24
———

9 4·31
+ 2·93
———

10 5·36
+ 1·29
———

11 3·87
+ 2·62
———

Write the total quantity.

2·75 l milk

3·46 l apple juice

3·5 l orange squash

1·92 l pineapple juice

2·09 l lemon squash

12 apple juice and milk

13 pineapple juice, lemon squash, orange squash

14 milk and lemon squash

15 apple juice, pineapple juice, orange squash

16 lemon squash and orange squash

17 orange squash, lemon squash, milk

How many ways are there of filling in these missing numbers? 3·☐ 6 + 1·☐ ☐ = 5

I can add numbers with two decimal places

Adding

Find the answer to these additions. You might calculate like this, or you might choose another method.

1. 5·06 + 3·7 + 2·85 =

2. 6·72 + 3·85 =

3. 4·8 + 2·05 + 0·87 =

4. 2·68 + 4·93 + 1·76 =

5. 5·76 + 3·8 =

6. 5·36 + 4·4 + 3·12 =

7. 3·57 + 8·2 + 7·4 =

8. 6·18 + 3·12 =

```
1.    1 2
         5·0 6
         3·7
    +    2·8 5
      1 1·6 1
         1 1
```

Each passenger has three bags. Find the weight of each person's bags.

9. 5·72 kg   6·84 kg   3·25 kg

10. 4·97 kg   6·34 kg   5·12 kg

11. 6·79 kg   4·38 kg   7·84 kg

12. 2·89 kg   6·38 kg   4·64 kg

13. 5·64 kg   7·92 kg   4·18 kg

14. 3·64 kg   4·93 kg   5·78 kg

The luggage limit is 20 kg. How much more can each passenger carry?

I can add numbers with two decimal places

Adding

£28·73

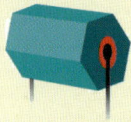 Tombola  Teas

£15·17

£15·30

 Splat the Rat

£7·08

Weight of the Cake

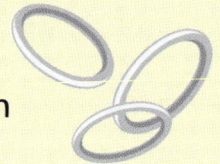

£32·09

White Elephant

£27·49

 Greasy Pole

£3·50

Hoop-lah

After a village fair the takings are added. Write the totals for:

1 White Elephant, Hoop-lah and Splat the Rat

2 Tombola, Greasy Pole, Weight of the Cake and Teas

3 White Elephant, Splat the Rat and Weight of the Cake

4 Tombola, Greasy Pole, Hoop-lah and Teas

5 Teas, Splat the rat, Tombola and Greasy Pole

6 White Elephant, Greasy Pole and Tombola

7 Weight of the cake, Hoop-lah, Teas and Tombola

8 Splat the Rat, Weight of the Cake, White Elephant and Hoop-lah

9 Three cakes weigh 3·75 kg, 2·18 kg and 1·9 kg. Find their total weight.

10 Shola buys a brass teapot (£4·45) a hat stand (£5·69) and an egg beater (85p). How much does she pay the White Elephant stall? How much change does she get from £20?

11 Jim spends £2·87 on the Tombola, £1·75 on the Hoop-lah and 76p climbing the Greasy Pole. How much does he spend in total?

Write your own word problem set at the village fair.

I can add numbers with two decimal places

Adding

Copy and complete.
Write an estimate first.

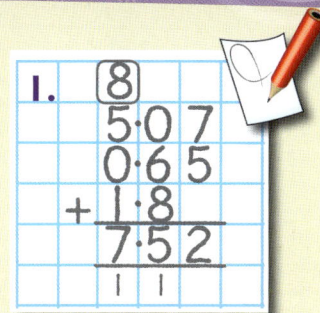

```
1.    (8)
      5·07
      0·65
    + 1·8
      7·52
      1 1
```

1   5·07 + 0·65 + 1·8 =

2   3·75 + 4·86 + 0·07 =

3   4·08 + 3·9 + 4·24 =

4   1·4 + 3·65 + 0·79 =

5   6·3 + 4·09 + 3·27 =

6   6·09 + 1·8 + 4·06 =

7   5·1 + 3·7 + 6·08 =

8   3·28 + 7·07 + 2·8 =

$$\square.\square\square + \square.\square\square + \square.\square\square = 10$$

Find some ways of filling the boxes, for example: 2·53 + 3·12 + 4·35 = 10
Can you find some ways in which no digit is used more than once?

True or false?

10
Adding three 2-place decimal numbers always results in an answer greater than 4.

11
Three lots of £1·99 is equal to twice £2·99.

9
6·54 + 3·21 is double 1·23 + 4·56.

Adding

1 Choose three CDs. Find the total cost. Do this 10 times. Write an estimate first.

POP CLASSICS £4·59

£5·68

£9·87

£7·38

£7·64

£5·57

```
 1.  £ 2 4
     £   9 · 8 7
     £   5 · 6 8
   + £   7 · 3 8
     £ 2 2 · 9 3
           1 2
```

2 Which three CDs cost the most? How much do they cost?

3 Which three CDs cost the least? How much do they cost?

> I bought two CDs for £14·46. Which CDs did I buy?

4 The men's long jump record is 8·95 m. The women's record is 7·52 m. If these were added together how far would this be?

5 Hilda bought a tent for £38·75 and a sleeping bag for £29·65. How much change did she have from £100?

6 Gita lives 4·8 km from Ghopal. Ghopal lives 5·6 km from Umesh, who lives 6·5 km from Basanti. How far must Gita go to visit them all?

Copy and complete.

7 14·68 + 25·59 =

8 23·95 + 36·87 =

9 48·84 + 36·97 =

10 55·97 + 43·85 =

11 12·59 + 8 + 7·3 =

12 14·53 + 9·17 =

13 3·82 + 10·37 + 1·66 =

14 4·25 + 12·68 + 3·27 =

I can add numbers with two decimal places

Adding

Fill in the missing numbers.

```
    3 6·4 7
  +   5·6 9
    4 2·1 6
      I I I
```
1.

1
```
    3 6·4 7
  +   5·□ 9
   □□·1 □
     I I I
```

2
```
   □□ 7·8 5
  + 1 7·7 6
   1 3□·□□
      I I I
```

3
```
    1 6·5 8
  + 4 3·□ 7
   □□·6 □
       I
```

4
```
    2 7·6 3
  +  □·4 2
    3 2·0 □
      I I
```

5
```
    1 8·□ 2
  + 1 6·3 8
   □□·3 □
     I I I
```

6
```
    4 2·8 9
  + 1□·2 □
    □ 2·□ 3
      I I I
```

7
```
    4 7·□ 6
  + □ 1·2 9
    6□·6 □
        I
```

8
```
    6 1·2 7
  + 1 2·□ 6
   □□·1 □
      I I
```

9
```
    □ 7·8 5
  + 2 2·3 1
    6□·□□
      I I
```

10
```
    1 2·3 8
  +   9·□ 2
   □□·8 □
     I    I
```

11
```
    1□·2 7
  + 2 4·9 6
    □ 3·□□
     I I  I
```

12
```
    2 1·6 5
  + 1 8·□ 8
   □□·4 □
     I I  I
```

13
```
    3 2·7 9
  +  □·7 3
    3 7·5 □
      I I
```

14
```
    2 7·3 4
  + 1 6·□ 3
   □□·1 □
      I I
```

15
```
    □ 4·3 8
  + 2 7·4 6
    8□·□□
      I    I
```

16
```
    6 7·5 4
  +   8·□ 5
   □□·4 □
      I I
```

Use one each of the number cards 0–9.
Arrange six of them like this:

```
  □·□□
+ □·□□
```

Try to make the total as near to 10 as possible.
Can you reach 10 exactly?

I can add with hundredths

Subtracting

Find the weight of letters left in the postman's van after 1 hour. You might calculate like this, or you might choose another method.

$$
\begin{array}{r}
1. \quad 8\overset{7\,6}{\cancel{7}}.\overset{70}{\cancel{5}}6 \\
-\ 1\ 8.7\ 4 \\
\hline
6\ 8.8\ 2\ \text{kg}
\end{array}
$$

1
start: 87·56 kg
delivered: 18·74 kg

2
start: 96·3 kg
delivered: 27·8 kg

3
start: 72·4 kg
delivered: 38·6 kg

4
start: 84·2 kg
delivered: 19·6 kg

5
start: 63·29 kg
delivered: 27·64 kg

6
start: 83·6 kg
delivered: 47·9 kg

7
start: 93·73 kg
delivered: 34·81 kg

8
start: 74·3 kg
delivered: 16·6 kg

9
start: 62·48 kg
delivered: 25·75 kg

10 Work with a partner. Choose three calculations.
Check your partner's work by adding.

Start with a 1-decimal place number
with repeating digits, for example: 545·4.
Subtract a 1-decimal place number,
also with repeating digits, for example: 272·7.
Look at the answer.
Repeat this process – look for different patterns.

I can do subtraction with units, tenths and hundredths

Subtracting

Write how much each T-shirt is reduced by. You might calculate like this, or you might choose another method.

1.

$$£3.23$$
$$£1.86 + £0.14 = £2.00$$
$$£2.00 + £1.23 = £3.23$$
$$£1.37$$

1 £1.86 ~~£3.23~~

2 £2.78 ~~£4.35~~

3 £1.76 ~~£2.34~~

4 £1.88 ~~£3.21~~

5 £2.96 ~~£4.22~~

6 £3.75 ~~£5.43~~

7 £2.86 ~~£4.25~~

8 £1.79 ~~£3.32~~

9 £3.87 ~~£5.34~~

You save £1·25 on a T-shirt. What could the original and the sale prices be?

Copy and complete.

10   £ 4·7 6
   − £ 2·4 8
   _____

11   £ 8·2 7
   − £ 4·7 3
   _____

12   £ 7·6 3
   − £ 3·2 6
   _____

13   £ 6·5 4
   − £ 3·4 8
   _____

14   £ 5·4 2
   − £ 3·9 1
   _____

15   £ 3·5 6
   − £ 2·7 4
   _____

16   £ 6·7 8
   − £ 3·4 9
   _____

17   £ 8·2 6
   − £ 5·4 1
   _____

I can do subtractions involving numbers with two decimal places

Subtracting

Hint: You might calculate like this, or you might choose another method.

1.			£4·60	
£2·80 + £0·20 = £3·00				
£3·00 + £1·60 = £4·60				
			£1·80	

How much more has:

1 Kelly than Sunil   **2** Sunil than Becky   **3** Lin Yao than Aleesha

4 Aleesha than Becky   **5** Kelly than Aleesha   **6** Lin Yao than Kelly?

Kelly    Sunil    Lin Yao    Aleesha    Becky

£4·60   £2·80   £5·10   £3·70   £1·90

How much more have:

7 Kelly and Sunil than Aleesha and Becky

8 Kelly and Lin Yao than Sunil and Aleesha?

How much in the purse now?

9  £6·08   **10**  £8·07   **11**  £7·04   **12**  £6·06

Spends £3·98   Spends £6·96   Spends £5·87   Spends £3·97

13  £5·03   **14**  £6·05   **15**  £4·02   **16**  £8·09

Spends £2·86   Spends £4·94   Spends £1·88   Spends £5·98

Exactly how many times can £9·99 be subtracted from £100? What is left at the end?

I can do subtractions involving numbers with two decimal places

Find the difference between each pair of children's savings. You might calculate like this, or you might choose another method. Write an estimate first.

```
1.   £6
   £11·38
 - £  4·86
```

Jimmy
£4·86

Sean
£13·19

Maya
£5·37

Loga
£11·38

Winston
£7·92

Choy
£12·74

1 Jimmy and Loga
2 Sean and Maya
3 Sean and Winston
4 Winston and Loga
5 Winston and Choy
6 Sean and Jimmy
7 Maya and Jimmy
8 Winston and Jimmy
9 Loga and Choy

Create a subtraction like this: ☐·☐☐ – ☐·☐☐
You may only use a digit once. Aim for an answer near 5.

Write the amount left to pay.

10
£8·62
£3·87 paid

11
£16·83
£7·96 paid

12
£19·23
£2·89 paid

13
£13·42
£2·89 paid

14
£16·83
£4·97 paid

15
£9·77
£3·98 paid

Subtracting

This is Lucy's homework. Check it for mistakes.
Write out correctly any that she got wrong.

1
$$\begin{array}{r} {}^{1}\cancel{2}\,{}^{1}\cancel{2}\,\cancel{6}\,{}^{1}3 \\ -\quad 8\ 8\ 4 \\ \hline 1\ 3\ 7\ 9 \end{array}$$

2
$$\begin{array}{r} \cancel{1}\,{}^{1}3\,\cancel{4}\,{}^{1}2 \\ -\quad 7\ 8\ 9 \\ \hline 6\ 5\ 3 \end{array}$$

3
$$\begin{array}{r} {}^{2}\cancel{3}\,{}^{1}4\,\cancel{2}\,{}^{1}3 \\ -\quad 6\ 5\ 7 \\ \hline 2\ 7\ 6\ 6 \end{array}$$

4
$$\begin{array}{r} {}^{5}\cancel{6}\,{}^{2}\cancel{3}\,\cancel{2}\,{}^{1}4 \\ -\quad 7\ 9\ 5 \\ \hline 5\ 5\ 3\ 9 \end{array}$$

5
$$\begin{array}{r} {}^{3}\cancel{4}\,{}^{1}\cancel{2}\,\cancel{5}\,{}^{1}3 \\ -\quad 6\ 8\ 4 \\ \hline 3\ 5\ 6\ 9 \end{array}$$

6
$$\begin{array}{r} {}^{2}\cancel{3}\,6\,{}^{3}\cancel{4}\,2 \\ -\quad 7\ 7\ 8 \\ \hline 2\ 9\ 6\ 5 \end{array}$$

Find the missing numbers.

7
$$\begin{array}{r} 1\ 2 \cdot 3\ 4 \\ -\quad ▨ \cdot 7\ ▨ \\ \hline 4 \cdot ▨\ 6 \end{array}$$

8
$$\begin{array}{r} 2\ 4 \cdot 5\ 1 \\ -\quad 6 \cdot ▨\ ▨ \\ \hline ▨\ ▨ \cdot 1\ 5 \end{array}$$

9
$$\begin{array}{r} 1\ 9 \cdot 6\ 3 \\ -\quad 7 \cdot 8\ ▨ \\ \hline ▨\ ▨ \cdot ▨\ 8 \end{array}$$

10
$$\begin{array}{r} 1\ 7 \cdot 2\ 9 \\ -\quad ▨ \cdot 6\ ▨ \\ \hline 1\ 1 \cdot ▨\ 5 \end{array}$$

11
$$\begin{array}{r} 2\ 1 \cdot 6\ 4 \\ -\quad 7 \cdot ▨\ ▨ \\ \hline ▨\ ▨ \cdot 8\ 1 \end{array}$$

12
$$\begin{array}{r} 1\ 5 \cdot 8\ 3 \\ -\quad 4 \cdot ▨\ ▨ \\ \hline ▨\ ▨ \cdot 2\ 6 \end{array}$$

13
$$\begin{array}{r} 2\ 3 \cdot 7\ 5 \\ -\quad 8 \cdot ▨\ ▨ \\ \hline ▨\ ▨ \cdot 7\ 8 \end{array}$$

14
$$\begin{array}{r} 1\ 8 \cdot 3\ 4 \\ -\quad ▨ \cdot 3\ ▨ \\ \hline 1\ 2 \cdot ▨\ 8 \end{array}$$

Write a 4-digit number with identical digits.　　2222
Write a 3-digit number with identical digits.　　666
The size of the digits in the second number must
be larger than the digits in the first number.
Take away the smaller from the larger number.　　2222 − 666
Repeat. Look for patterns.

I can do subtractions involving numbers with two decimal places

Multiplying

Copy and complete.

1.

	4	0·6
3	12	1·8

12·0 + 1·8 = 13·8

$3 \times 4·6 = 13·8$

1

	4	0·6
3		

2

	2	0·7
4		

3

	3	0·4
7		

4

	5	0·9
8		

5

	6	0·8
6		

6

	7	0·4
9		

7

	6	0·3
5		

8

	7	0·2
7		

9

	5	0·6
6		

Multiply each number by 7.

10 6 · 3
11 4 · 6
12 7 · 4
13 9 · 7
14 5 · 8
15 8 · 3
16 5 · 4
17 8 · 4
18 5 · 6
19 3 · 2

10.

	6	0·3
7	42	2·1

42·0 + 2·1 = 44·1

$7 \times 6·3 = 44·1$

Try this multiplication: $7 \times \boxed{}·\boxed{} = 20$. How close can you get?

Multiplying

Find the multiplication shown by each grid.

1.

	6	0·3
4	24	1·2

240
+ 1·2
25·2

1

4	24	1·2

2

6	42	2·4

3

7	21	6·3

4

8	40	6·4

5

3	24	2·1

6

6	42	1·8

Write the height of each stack of tins.

7.

	4	0·3
6	24	1·8

240
+ 1·8
25·8

7 4·3 cm — squid rings — 6 tins

8 6·8 cm — mussels — 4 tins

9 3·8 cm — MACKEREL fillets — 7 tins

10 4·7 cm — TUNA — 8 tins

11 5·2 cm — SALMON CHUNKS Ocean — 6 tins

12 3·4 cm — Ocean SARDINES — 9 tins

My stack of tins is 32·9 cm high. Which of the tins above could it be made from? Invent a question like this for your friend to answer.

I can use the grid method to multiply units and tenths

Complete these multiplications.
You might calculate like this or you
might choose another method.

1.	7	×	4	·6	7 × 4·0 = 2 8 ·0
					7 × 0·6 = 4 ·2
					7 × 4·6 = 3 2 ·2

1   7 × 4·6 =

2   4 × 7·4 =

3   3 × 8·6 =

4   8 × 4·9 =

5   6 × 5·7 =

6   9 × 3·8 =

7   7 × 6·4 =

8   8 × 9·4 =

9   6 × 7·9 =

10   9 × 5·2 =

11   7 × 3·6 =

12   8 × 5·7 =

Write the weight of each.

13   6 packs

4·2 kg

14   4 packs

2·7 kg

15   7 packs

3·8 kg

16   8 packs of cola
1·6 kg each

17   7 packs of tonic
2·4 kg each

18   5 packs of smoothies
6·8 kg each

19   8 packs of juice
4·9 kg each

20   3 packs of squash
5·7 kg each

21   9 packs of milk
3·3 kg each

Multiply ☐ · ☐ × ☐

What is the largest answer you can make, using the digits 6, 7 and 8?
What is the smallest answer you can make?

Multiplying

Complete these multiplications. You might calculate like this, or you might choose another method. Then use a calculator to check by dividing.

1.	9	×	4·7	9 × 4	=...
				9 × 0·7	=...
				9 × 4·7	=...
	4	2·3	÷ 9	=...	

1 9 × 4·7 =

2 8 × 3·4 =

3 6 × 5·2 =

4 7 × 8·6 =

5 4 × 9·3 =

6 5 × 4·3 =

7 8 × 3·9 =

8 6 × 7·6 =

9 7 × 6·4 =

Correct any errors.

Investigate the perimeter of regular polygons that have a side of length 4·7 cm.

Estimate the largest and smallest of each set. Complete the multiplications and put them in order. Were you correct?

10 3·6 × 4   5·2 × 5   4·3 × 7   2·8 × 9

11 4·2 × 6   7·9 × 3   5·8 × 4   2·7 × 8

12 6·3 × 5   4·4 × 7   9·2 × 3   2·8 × 9

13 4·9 × 4   9·3 × 2   4·2 × 5   2·7 × 8

14 8·7 × 6   5·4 × 9   6·6 × 8   7·3 × 7

I can multiply units and tenths

Multiplying

Find the answer to these multiplications. You might calculate like this, or you might choose another method. Write an estimate first.

1	(28)	2	(40)	3	( )
	4·3		5·2		3·6
×	7	×	8	×	4
	———		———		———

4	$3 \times 5·8$	5	$9 \times 6·4$	6	$6 \times 7·8$	7	$4 \times 2·9$
8	$3 \times 7·7$	9	$5 \times 4·6$	10	$3 \times 6·3$	11	$5 \times 2·8$
12	$4 \times 5·4$	13	$3 \times 6·6$	14	$5 \times 3·7$	15	$4 \times 4·3$

These children recorded how long it took to write their name. How long do they take to write their name the given number of times?

16 Guy
2·7 seconds
8 times

17 Tracey
5·6 seconds
4 times

18 Catherine
9·2 seconds
7 times

19 Ilesh
6·4 seconds
5 times

20 Elizabeth
9·4 seconds
6 times

21 Davinder
8·7 seconds
3 times

22 Tim
1·9 seconds
7 times

23 Sunam
4·7 seconds
6 times

24 Yasmin
7·3 seconds
4 times

Work with a partner. Use a stopwatch to find how long it takes to write your name and address. Use multiplication to find how long it would take to write it 12 times.

I can multiply units and tenths

Multiplying

Hint: You might calculate like this, or you might choose another method.

1.

	4	0·5	0·06		12·0
3	12	15	0·18 +		1·5
					0·18
					13·68

£8·72

£1·98

£3·68

£4·56

£7·85

£5·74

£2·75

Write the cost of:

1 3 pairs of gloves   **2** 4 bobble hats   **3** 5 pairs of shorts

4 8 T-shirts   **5** 3 caps   **6** 6 pairs of flip-flops

7 8 pairs of socks   **8** 4 pairs each of socks and gloves

You can buy any two items. Investigate how many of each you can buy with £30.

Complete these multiplications.

9 $3 \times 1·26 =$ **10** $4 \times 2·57 =$ **11** $5 \times 4·36 =$

12 $8 \times 7·42 =$ **13** $9 \times 3·87 =$ **14** $4 \times 8·64 =$

15 $7 \times 3·92 =$ **16** $6 \times 4·38 =$ **17** $9 \times 5·28 =$

I can multiply with tenths and hundredths

Multiplying

Nine children created a decimal multiplication. Find their answers. Whose answer is nearest to 20? Whose is second nearest?

1.	5	×	4·3 2	
	5	×	4	=
	5	×	0·3	=
	5	×	0·0 2	=
	5	×	4·3 2	=

Hint: You might calculate like this, or you might choose another method.

1 Josh $5 \times 4 \cdot 3 \ 2$

2 Natalie $6 \times 3 \cdot 7 \ 8$

3 Amit $2 \times 9 \cdot 4 \ 1$

4 Ben $3 \times 6 \cdot 7 \ 5$

5 Susie $4 \times 5 \cdot 2 \ 3$

6 Lucy $7 \times 2 \cdot 8 \ 5$

7 Narinder $8 \times 2 \cdot 2 \ 3$

8 Paul $9 \times 1 \cdot 8 \ 4$

9 Ghopal $4 \times 4 \cdot 7 \ 2$

Calculate the perimeters of these regular polygons.

10 a square of side 3·24 cm

11 a pentagon of side 4·56 cm

12 an octagon of side 5·73 cm

13 an equilateral triangle of side 9·28 cm

14 a hexagon of side 4·47 cm

15 a nonagon of side 6·83 cm

16 a hexagon of side 8·67 cm

17 an octagon of side 6·84 cm

A shape shop sells plastic regular polygons. All the sides of the polygons are 3·69 cm long. Investigate the perimeter of the different polygons up to 10 sides.

I can multiply with tenths and hundredths

Multiplying

Choose three of the four digits to make the multiplication correct.

1

| 2 | 3 |
| 4 | 7 |

$$\square \cdot \square \square \\ \times \quad 6 \\ \overline{2\ 8 \cdot 3\ 2}$$

2

| 3 | 4 |
| 6 | 8 |

$$\square \cdot \square \square \\ \times \quad 5 \\ \overline{1\ 9 \cdot 2\ 0}$$

3

| 4 | 2 |
| 5 | 3 |

$$\square \cdot \square \square \\ \times \quad 7 \\ \overline{3\ 0 \cdot 2\ 4}$$

4

| 7 | 8 |
| 6 | 9 |

$$\square \cdot \square \square \\ \times \quad 8 \\ \overline{5\ 5 \cdot 1\ 2}$$

5

| 4 | 7 |
| 6 | 5 |

$$\square \cdot \square \square \\ \times \quad 9 \\ \overline{5\ 1 \cdot 8\ 4}$$

6

| 5 | 7 |
| 6 | 8 |

$$\square \cdot \square \square \\ \times \quad 4 \\ \overline{3\ 0 \cdot 3\ 2}$$

$3 \cdot 27 \times 4 = 6 \cdot 54 \times 2$

Can you find other pairs of multiplications like this:

$\square \cdot \square \square \times \square$ that have the same answer?

7 Jim has 8 pieces of fencing, each 1·75 m long. He needs to build a fence 21 m long. How short is his fence, and how many more pieces must he buy?

8 Rashida buys a fish tank for £35·70 and 8 fish at £2·76 each. She only has £45·30 in her purse. How much more will she need to borrow?

9 Kate and 6 of her friends are going on a train journey. The tickets cost £6·38 each. How much change will they have from £50?

I can multiply with tenths and hundredths

Dividing

Find the answer to these divisions. You might calculate like this, or you might choose another method.

1

$53·2 \div 4 =$

$\begin{array}{l} - 40 \\ \hline 13·2 \\ -12 \\ \hline 1·2 \\ -1·2 \\ \hline \end{array}$

$= ⑩ \times 4$

$= ③ \times 4$

$= ⓪·③ \times 4$

2

$55·2 \div 3 =$

$\begin{array}{l} - 30 \\ \hline 25·2 \\ \hline \\ \hline \end{array}$

$= ⑩ \times 3$

$= ⑧ \times 3$

3

$88·2 \div 6 =$

$\begin{array}{l} - 60 \\ \hline \\ \hline \\ \hline \end{array}$

$= ⑩ \times 6$

4 $52·8 \div 4 =$

5 $36·9 \div 3 =$

6 $75·5 \div 5 =$

Some marathon runners have agreed to share the running. Each will run the same distance. How far does one person run?

7 4 runners 68·8 km

8 3 runners 44·1 km

9 4 runners 45·2 km

10 3 runners 70·8 km

11 4 runners 90·8 km

12 3 runners 41·7 km

13 6 runners 76·2 km

14 3 runners 80·4 km

15 4 runners 75·2 km

In questions 7–15, the race route is increased to 100 km. How much further must each runner go than they had planned?

Dividing

The total weight of vegetables is shown. Each of the vegetables in a set weighs the same. How much does one vegetable weigh? You might calculate like this, or you might choose another method.

```
 1.      8 4·6 g
      −  6 0        (20)× 3
         2 4·6
      −  2 4          (8)× 3
           0·6
      −    0·6      (0·2)× 3
             0
         8 4·6 ÷ 3 = 2 8·2 g
```

1

84·6 g

2

81·6 g

3

79·2 g

4

88·5 g

5

90·3 g

6

35·2 g

7

90·8 g

8

88·2 g

9

67·6 g

Choose three divisions. Check each by multiplying the answer by the divisor.

With a partner, discuss approximately how many of each vegetable there are in 1 kilogram.

Complete these divisions.

10 $58·8 ÷ 4 =$ **11** $70·8 ÷ 3 =$ **12** $73·2 ÷ 6 =$

13 $94·4 ÷ 8 =$ **14** $98·4 ÷ 6 =$ **15** $96·9 ÷ 3 =$

16 $86·4 ÷ 4 =$ **17** $82·2 ÷ 6 =$ **18** $95·6 ÷ 4 =$

I can divide numbers where the answer has one decimal place

Dividing

Choose how to solve these calculations:

1 2·1 ÷ 3 =   2 7·2 ÷ 8 =   3 5·6 ÷ 7 =   4 4·8 ÷ 6 =

5 82·5 ÷ 5 =   6 35·4 ÷ 6 =   7 49·2 ÷ 6 =   8 52·2 ÷ 9 =

9 55·5 ÷ 3 =   10 31·6 ÷ 4 =   11 41·6 ÷ 8 =   12 59·4 ÷ 6 =

13 98·4 ÷ 6 =   14 23·6 ÷ 4 =   15 47·4 ÷ 6 =   16 32·2 ÷ 7 =

Choose three of the divisions. Check your answer
by multiplying it by the divisor.

Calculate these divisions in your head:
29 ÷ 2, 56 ÷ 5, 6 ÷ 4.

Compare your answer with your partner's.
Do you have the same answers?

If not why is there a difference?

Choose how to solve these calculations:

17 457·8 ÷ 6 =   18 306·0 ÷ 4 =   19 417·4 ÷ 2 =

20 415·2 ÷ 4 =   21 428·1 ÷ 3 =   22 107·2 ÷ 4 =

23 138·0 ÷ 4 =   24 424·2 ÷ 6 =   25 500·0 ÷ 8 =

I can divide numbers where the answer has one decimal place

Dividing

Do these divisions. You might calculate like this, or you might choose another method.

```
1.    5·2 4
    − 4          ①× 4
      1·2 4
    − 1·2        0·3 × 4
      0·0 4
      0·0 4      0·0 1 × 4
          0
    5·2 4 ÷ 4 = 1·3 1
```

1   $5·24 ÷ 4 =$

2   $3·15 ÷ 5 =$

3   $4·16 ÷ 4 =$

4   $8·24 ÷ 2 =$

5   $12·39 ÷ 3 =$

6   $7·68 ÷ 4 =$

7   $14·77 ÷ 7 =$

8   $7·56 ÷ 6 =$

9   $5·45 ÷ 5 =$

Three children used the same four digits to make a decimal division. Whose answer is closest to 1?

10   Josh $6 · 2 8 ÷ 4$

11   Natalie $2 · 6 8 ÷ 4$

12   Suzie $4 · 6 8 ÷ 2$

Use these numbers: and a decimal point.   6   8   2   5

Make up some divisions. What is the highest answer you can get? And the lowest?

Can you make an answer close to 1? How close?

I can use division methods I learnt for whole numbers when dividing decimal numbers

Dividing

These windows are regular polygons. Calculate the length of side of each window. You might calculate like this, or you might choose another method.

1.

$$\begin{array}{r} 7\cdot28\,\text{m} \\ -\;4 \end{array} \qquad = ① \quad \times 4$$

$$\begin{array}{r} 3\cdot28 \\ -\;3\cdot2 \end{array} \qquad = ⓪\!\cdot\!8 \quad \times 4$$

$$\begin{array}{r} 0\cdot08 \\ -\;0\cdot08 \\ \hline 0 \end{array} \qquad = ⓪\!\cdot\!02 \times 4$$

$$7\cdot28\,\text{m} \div 4 = 1\cdot82$$

1
P = 7·28 m

2
P = 8·22 m

3
P = 9·72 m

4
P = 6·95 m

Check each division by multiplying the answer by the divisor.

 In this window, the perimeter is 8·42 m. Three sides are of equal length. Explore the possible lengths of the sides.

Each day the painters cover the same length of fence. How much do they paint in a day?

5
82·02 m   3 days

6
73·84 m   4 days

7
68·2 m   5 days

8 89·74 m   1 week

9 96·42 m   3 days

10 70·68 m   6 days

11 84·92 m   4 days

12 87·08 m   1 week

13 79·38 m   3 days

I can use division methods I learnt for whole numbers when dividing decimal numbers, and I can explain how I do this

Dividing

Friends go out for a pizza, and split the bill equally. How much does each person pay? You could do these like you have done before or like the example here.

1.		8	3	4
4	3	3	3	6

1 £33·36
4 people

2 £18·84
3 people

3 £44·76
6 people

4 £76·24
8 people

5 £47·04
7 people

6 £25·41
3 people

To divide by a multiple of 10 you can use the clever way of dividing both numbers by 10, for example: 473·2 ÷ 30 = 47·32 ÷ 3. Use the trick to help with these divisions.

7 856·8 ÷ 40

8 883·8 ÷ 60

9 97·53 ÷ 30

10 886·9 ÷ 70

11 942·4 ÷ 80

12 975·6 ÷ 90

18·36 ÷ 0·3. Can you and your partner think of a trick to help you solve this division? What about 24·84 ÷ 0·04?

I can use division methods I learnt for whole numbers when dividing decimal numbers, and I can explain how I do this

Percentages of amounts

1   Calculate the volume of each fruit in a 750 ml smoothie:

5% of the smoothie is mashed banana

10% of the smoothie is pineapple juice

20% of the smoothie is mashed mango

65% of the smoothie is orange juice

If these quantities are doubled to make a 1·5 l size smoothie, what would the volume of each fruit be? What would the percentages of the fruits in the 1·5 l smoothie be?

2   Calculate the volume of each fruit in a 250 ml smoothie:

1% crushed cherries

2% mashed banana

5% orange juice

7% apple juice

10% crushed raspberries

15% crushed strawberries

60% bramble juice

The chef is making a new family size smoothie.
This is to be 2 l (2000 ml).
Help him by deciding the types of fruit, and the percentages and volume of fruit to go in the smoothie.

Percentages of amounts

1 Andrew receives £120 for his birthday. He spends 75% of this on a new music player. How much was the music player?

2 The school quiz team has scored 280 points in the competition. Copy and complete the table below to show how well each player did.

Name	Percentage	Number of points scored
Douglas	50%	
Ella		70
John	15%	
Kirsten		

Remember that everybody is different and we all have different health and eating requirements so these figures are not exact for everybody.

Girls between the ages of 9 and 13 should consume about 1900 calories daily, and boys of the same age need about 2400 calories every day.

These calories should come from a number of different food groups. The amount of calories that you should get from each food group is:

10 to 30 percent from protein

45 to 65 percent from carbohydrates

25 to 35 percent from fats

How many calories should boys and girls get from each food group in a day?

I can solve problems involving percentages of an amount

Percentages of amounts

Frugal's Strawberry Fizz contains 15% real fruit.
There are 1000 ml in a litre.
How much real fruit is there in a:

1 100 ml bottle

2 250 ml bottle

3 1·5 litre bottle?

Yogi's Fruit Yoghurt contains 9% real fruit.
How much real fruit is there in a:

4 150 g pot

5 400 g pot

6 700 g pot?

Ophrey's Organic Orange Juice contains 45% real fruit.
How much real fruit is there in a:

7 200 ml carton
8 750 ml carton
9 1·2 litre carton?

Petra's Pure Prune Juice contains 76% real fruit.
How much real fruit is there in a:

10 800 ml bottle
11 300 ml bottle
12 1·4 litre bottle?

Eric drinks 4 glasses of Ophrey's Organic Orange Juice a day which contains 35% real fruit.

The glasses are 50 ml each.

What is the volume of real fruit that he drinks each day?

What is the volume of real fruit that he drinks in a week?

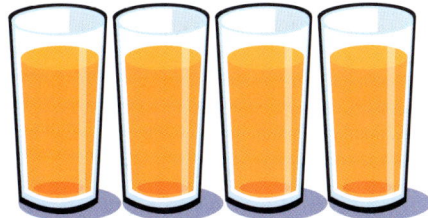

I can solve problems involving percentages of an amount

Percentage increase

What will the new weight be for each item?

1

Weight 200 g
25% extra

2

Weight 450 g
10% extra

3

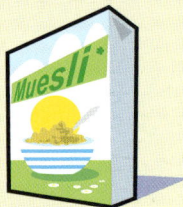

Weight 850 g
20% extra

4

Weight 560 g
30% extra

5

Weight 700 g
5% extra

6

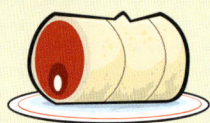

Weight 940 g
50% extra

7

Weight 650 g
40% extra

8

Weight 1020 g
5% extra

9 The pupils in Primary 6 bake cakes to raise money for charity. Their ingredients cost £7·60 for biscuits, £6·80 for scones, £15·40 for tray bakes, and £12·80 for sponge cakes.
They decide to charge 15% more than the ingredients cost for each item.
How much should they sell the items for?

10 These friends at Glen Ardbeg Athletics club have improved their personal records. Copy and complete the table to show their new records.

Name	Event	Previous record	Percentage increase	New record
Jamil	High jump	1·36 m	10%	
Hilary	Long jump	2·25 m	5%	
Katie	Shot putt	5·35 m	20%	

I can work out a new value after a percentage increase

Percentage decrease

FDP2.20b

What will be the new price for these items?

1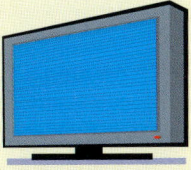
Price £600
25% off

2
Price £450
10% off

3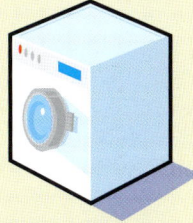
Price £480
20% off

4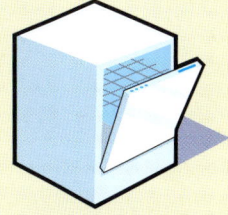
Price £360
30% off

5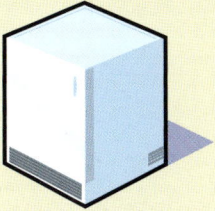
Price £790
5% off

6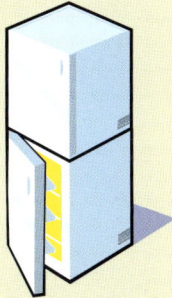
Price £965
50% off

7
Price £138
40% off

8
Price £88
5% off

9 Murraylawn Football Club are decreasing their season ticket prices. What will the new prices be?

Type of Ticket	Previous price	Percentage decrease	New price
Adult	£275	10%	
Child U12	£145	75%	
Youth U18	£165	20%	
OAP	£150	30%	
Family	£635	40%	

I can work out a new value after a percentage decrease

89

Percentage change

A vehicle dealership has a sale on. What are the new prices?

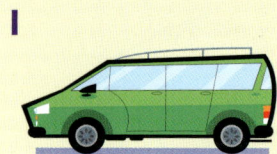

1
Price £6500
25% off

2
Price £4450
10% off

3
Price £3480
20% off

4
Price £4360
30% off

5
Price £1890
5% off

6
Price £7965
30% off

7
Price £2538
20% off

8
Price £8600
15% off

9 The following shows weather information for Glasgow in 2008.

Month	Jan	Feb	Mar	Apr	May	Jun	Jul	Aug	Sep	Oct	Nov	Dec
Average high °C	6	6	8	11	15	17	18	18	15	12	8	6
Rainfall mm	87	79	74	47	33	39	50	53	57	85	86	75

In 2009 some values changed. What were the 2009 figures for the months shown below?

Average high °C	May: increase 3%	Aug: decrease 2%	Nov: increase 4%
Rainfall mm	Mar: increase 6%	Jul: decrease 17%	Dec: decrease 7%

Catherine has £100 savings in a bank account. Each year this earns 5% interest which is added on to the savings. How much will she have after 2 years?

I can work out a new value after a percentage decrease or increase

Percentage calculations

1 Eight children got the following marks for their school work.
   Convert their marks to percentages.

Name	Spelling (out of 10)	Maths (out of 20)	General knowledge (out of 40)
Simona	6	14	20
Katie	7	15	10
Wai-Sen	10	12	25
Faye	3	8	26
Eshveer	5	16	34
James	9	13	38
Catherine	8	17	16
Andrew	2	11	28

1.

Name	Spelling	Maths	General knowledge
Simona	$\frac{6}{10}$ = 60%	$\frac{14}{20}$ = 70%	$\frac{20}{40}$ = 50%

2 Simona's best mark was in maths. In which subject did
   the other children do best?

Sean used a calculator to help him with his percentage problems. He had to increase £45 by 10% so he keyed in 4 5 x 1 · 1 and got the answer 4 9 · 5. He interpreted this as £49·50. Was his answer correct? Can you explain why his method works?

Percentage calculations

Write these fractions as percentages.

1. $\frac{1}{2} = 50\%$

1. $\frac{1}{2}$

2. $\frac{2}{10}$

3. $\frac{2}{5}$

4. $\frac{3}{4}$

5. $\frac{30}{60}$

6. $\frac{3}{12}$

7. $\frac{6}{8}$

8. $\frac{9}{12}$

9. There are 50 children in P4 and P5.
30 of them have school dinners.
What percentage is this of the whole?

10. A box can hold 80 pencils. There are
40 pencils in the box. What is this as a
percentage of the whole 80?

11. In a class of 20 children a survey was
carried out to find their favourite colours.
The results were:

Colour	Number of children
Red	8
Purple	4
Blue	6
Pink	2

Write the numbers of children who chose each
colour as a percentage of the whole class.

Ask 30 people which they prefer out of red, purple, blue
or pink. Write your results up as percentages. How do
they compare?

I can solve problems involving working out percentages

Percentage calculations

Wei, Tom and Abraham are taking part in an 80 mile sports challenge. Wei plans to cycle 50 miles, Tom will kayak for 20 miles and Abraham will run 10 miles.

1 What percentage of the distance will each person do?

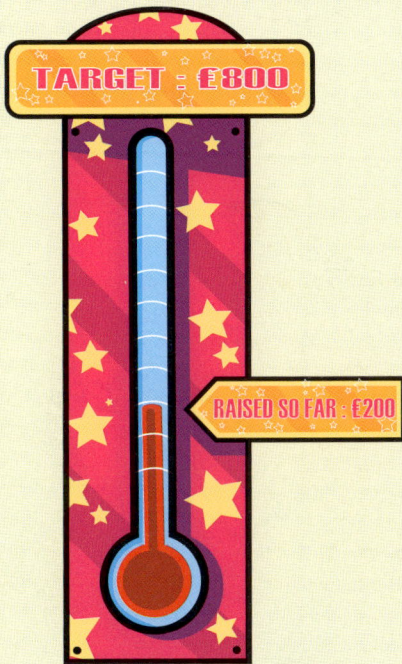

TARGET : £800

RAISED SO FAR : £200

They are raising money for charity and aim to make £800. What percentage of this target will they have raised when the total is:

2 £400   **3** £600   **4** £800?

5 They finally reached £800. Wei had raised £160, Tom had raised £320 and Abraham had raised the rest. What percentage of the total did they each raise?

6 Next year the challenge will be for 90 miles. How might they share out the distance to be covered this time? What percentage of the distance will each person do?

If they had raised £1000 how could that be shown as a percentage of their target?

Word problems

Monica carries out an investigation into the colours of sweets in a packet. There are 30 sweets altogether in the packet.

She discovers:

3 of the sweets are blue

0·4 of the packet is red sweets

0·3 of the packet is yellow sweets

20% of the packet is green sweets.

1   Which colour is there most of?

2   Which colour is there least of?

Carry out your own investigation into items with different colours, for example boxes of coloured paper clips or beads. What do you find out?

Here is the nutritional information on two packets of biscuits.

Nutritional information	In a 10 g Bon biscuit	Nutritional information	In a 15 g Oaty oat biscuit
Protein	1·1 g	Protein	0·6 g
Carbohydrate	8·3 g	Carbohydrate	9·6 g
Fat	3·1 g	Fat	4·7 g
Fibre	0·6 g	Fibre	0·9 g
Salt	0·1 g	Salt	0·3 g

3   The biscuits are different weights. How can you compare the information that you have about the biscuits accurately?

4   Write four facts comparing the nutritional information of the two biscuits.

I can solve problems involving decimal fractions and percentages

Calculation investigations

1 What could my number be, when all of the following statements are true?

When I divide by 2 I get no remainder.

When I divide by 5 I get a remainder of 4.

When I divide by 9 I get a remainder of 1.

What is the question when the following numbers are the answers?

2 4 r 3

3 $2\frac{1}{2}$

4 3·4

What could the questions be when the following answers are rounded like this?

5 3·4 is rounded to 4.

6 3·4 is rounded to 3.

7 3·4 is rounded to 3·5.

Show as many different ways of calculating this answer as possible:

12·48 ÷ 4

Share these with a partner.
Who has found the most different methods?
Which method did you prefer? Is it different to the method your partner preferred?

I can solve problems involving decimal fractions

Heinemann active maths

Author Team:
Peter Gorrie, Lynda Keith, Lynne McClure and Amy Sinclair

Heinemann

Part of Pearson

Heinemann is an imprint of Pearson Education Limited, a company incorporated in England and Wales, having its registered office at Edinburgh Gate, Harlow, Essex, CM20 2JE. Registered company number: 872828

www.pearsonschools.co.uk

Heinemann is a registered trademark of Pearson Education Limited

First published 2010

14 13 12 11 10
10 9 8 7 6 5 4 3 2 1

British Library Cataloguing in Publication Data
A catalogue record for this book is available from the British Library

ISBN 978 0 4350 4366 7

Typeset by Debbie Oatley @ room9design
Illustrations © Harcourt Education Limited 2006-2007, Pearson Education Limited 2010
Illustrated by Piers Baker, Fred Blunt, Emma Brownjohn, Tom Cole, Jonathan Edwards, Stephen Elford, Andy Hammond, John Haslam, Andrew Hennessey, Nigel Kitching, Sim Marriott, Q2A Media, Debbie Oatley, Andrew Painter, Tom Percival, Mark Ruffle, Anthony Rule, Eric Smith, Dale Sullivan and Gary Swift
Cover design by Pearson Education Limited
Cover illustration Volker Beisler © Pearson Education Limited
Printed in the UK by Scotprint

Acknowledgements

Every effort has been made to contact copyright holders of material reproduced in this book. Any omissions will be rectified in subsequent printings if notice is given to the publishers.